JACK SHELTON'S
HOW TO ENJOY 1 TO 10
PERFECT DAYS IN
SAN FRANCISCO

JACK SHELTON'S HOW TO ENJOY 1 TO 10 PERFECT DAYS IN SAN FRANCISCO

Completely updated and expanded by

JACK R. JUHASZ

FOURTH EDITION

Edited by Dale Richards

SHELTON PUBLICATIONS
BOX 391
SAUSALITO, CALIF. 94966

Library of Congress Catalog Card Number: 86-090388
ISBN 0-918742-03-X

PRINTED IN THE UNITED STATES OF AMERICA

SHELTON PUBLICATIONS
Box 391
Sausalito, California 94966
(415) 332-1165

Contents

Introduction

When Jack Shelton and I planned the very first edition of this book nearly twenty-five years ago, we both wanted to make it as interesting and as unique as the city which is its subject—San Francisco.

Jack, a transplanted New Yorker, loved San Francisco passionately because to him it represented a less hectic life-style in more beautiful and congenial surroundings. I, as a native San Franciscan, loved it as all natives love and cherish it.

Together, we set out to create a guide book that would put onto paper exactly what we would recommend to you if you were a close friend visiting here for the very first time. To give you the very best this marvelous city has to offer, no matter how short your stay.

Therefore, the first day, for example, presents what we would recommend you do if you had only one day to spend here. If you had only two days, we would go on to suggest the second day's activities and so forth.

Because the scheduling involves many arbitrary decisions on our part, times and days are set purely as a guide and should not inhibit you. Switch things around to suit yourself.

We begin with a day-to-day schedule covering one complete, perfect week basically in the city itself. Then for the remaining days, we offer two-, three- and four-day suggested trips to areas easily reached from San Francisco: Carmel-Monterey and Hearst Castle, the Mendocino Coast, Yosemite National Park, and—new to this edition—the Napa Valley.

Since dining out is the favorite pastime for native and visitor alike in San Francisco, great emphasis has been placed on restaurant-going in this book. Even though San

Francisco is world famous as a "restaurant town," like all such cities it nevertheless possesses a substantial number of terrible "tourist traps." To make sure you not only avoid these but discover the truly fine restaurants (many of which do not advertise aggressively), each day's schedule gives you a variety of selections for both lunch and dinner. In addition, specific recommendations on what to order insure your getting the best each kitchen has to offer. In choosing these restaurants for you, we have drawn on our twenty years of experience as Bay Area restaurant critics.

What you will find are some fifty of our personal favorites—some famous, others obscure little "finds"—which will provide you with the finest and most interesting dining experiences in town. And when that "town" is San Francisco, it means some of the finest and most exciting dining anywhere! As with all other recommended activities, though, let your personal taste and budget be your guide. If you want to switch restaurant visits around or follow a special craving or whim, do so. And to help you do just that we have included a separate restaurant index, which lists all the restaurants reviewed in this book by both location and type of cuisine served.

Should you find yourself heading home with a lot left to see and experience, do not feel bad. Remember . . . there is no such thing as visiting San Francisco only once.

Jack R. Juhasz

PART ONE

One Perfect Week

in San Francisco

Your First Perfect Day Schedule

8:30 a.m. Board a Hyde Street cable car at Powell and Market Streets in front of Woolworth's.

9:00 a.m. Arrive at the last stop and have breakfast at the Buena Vista Cafe, corner of Beach and Hyde Streets.

10:00 a.m. After breakfast, stroll to Aquatic Park, the Maritime Museum, Hyde Street Pier, The Cannery and Fisherman's Wharf.

11:45 a.m. Hop a Powell Street cable car and either get off at Pacific Avenue for a "dim sum" lunch at a tiny Chinatown hideaway followed by a walk through Chinatown; or remain on board to Market Street and lunch in the breathtaking Garden Court of the historic Palace Hotel.

2:00 p.m. Pick up your rental car for the 49-Mile Drive, or take Gray Line's City Tour #1.

7:00 p.m. Cocktails at the Top of the Mark.

8:00 p.m. A short stroll around Nob Hill.

8:30 p.m. Luxurious French, exciting Californian or Hungarian with a view are your culinary choices for dinner tonight.

11:00 p.m. Take in the late show at the Venetian Room in TV's *Hotel* which is San Francisco's Fairmont.

2:00 a.m. If you are still up, a goodnight view of San Francisco from the top of Telegraph Hill; or a visit to a "jook house."

How to Spend One Perfect Day

in San Francisco

8:30 a.m. Do not have breakfast (or just have coffee) at your hotel. Find Market Street, which is easy since it is the main thoroughfare of downtown San Francisco, and look for the big Woolworth's store located at the beginning of Powell Street. Right in front of Woolworth's you will find what children and many adults would travel halfway around the world to see—the famous San Francisco cable cars. Board the Powell and Hyde Street one (look for a maroon sign on the roof) and, weather permitting, try to get an outside seat on the right-hand side (Woolworth's side).

By sitting on the outside section, you will be privileged to watch the gripman as he runs the car. You will quickly discover that cable car gripmen and fare collectors are a breed unto themselves with extraordinarily open personalities. During your over-the-hills ride, you may see them interrupt a flirtation with a pretty young passenger to chastise an impatient motorist with such remarks as, "You dare honk your horn at a national historical monument?" You cannot help noticing their special pride and warmth about being the ones who give life to "that historical monument," and they will readily answer any questions you may have about the cable car.

However, in case you are shy, let me explain that the cable car runs with the aid of a continuously moving cable (9½-miles-per-hour) located below the street. The street contains an open slot the entire length of the run, and the car has clamps which extend into the slot and fasten onto the cable below to propel the car forward. Releasing the grip stops the car. It cannot back up, but it does have a braking mechanism. In addition, the cable car triggers a device which causes traffic lights on hills to turn green as it approaches. Cross traffic stops so the car can make it to the top. Cable cars contain no electricity and the lights are operated by a battery.

Now, here we go up Powell Street, eight stops to the top of Nob Hill. From a right-hand seat on the cable car, you will get an exciting look down California Street past Chinatown to the Bay. Twisting your neck to look out the other side of the car will show you the famous Fairmont and Mark Hopkins Hotels, both of which you will see more closely later in the day.

Another few blocks—the gripman warns you to hang on as the car first swings left and then soon rounds another curve onto Hyde Street heading toward Russian Hill. Here, the car again starts climbing and in a few moments, you will see two of the most thrilling views in all the world. The first will present itself to you at the top of Lombard Street, "the crookedest street in the world." (Notice how the street curves several times around flower beds.) Your view will be eastward toward Telegraph Hill, capped with Coit Tower, and the Bay with the Bay Bridge connecting San Francisco to the East Bay. Soon, a turn of your head forward and slightly to the left will give you a panoramic view of the Golden Gate Bridge. Then a deep breath as the car goes down the hill—a glance at Alcatraz Island right in front of you and a feeling of relief when the car stops at its final destination, Beach Street. Here you will get off and find yourself in front of the Buena Vista Cafe, 2765 Hyde (474-5044; open weekdays from 9 a.m.; weekends from 8 a.m.). And even if the doors have just opened, do not be surprised if you find a line already formed.

9:00 a.m. Enter the Buena Vista Cafe, find a table overlooking the charming Victorian Park with its cable car turntable and the waterfront beyond, and immediately order (service can be slow when crowded) a fine, hearty breakfast with one of the Buena Vista world-famous Irish Coffees as a finale. Of course, if you have a few encores of this concoction, which was introduced to the United States in 1953 right on this spot, your first perfect day in San Francisco may start and finish at the Buena Vista. However, I can think of far worse fates!

To begin your breakfast, ask for another B.V. favorite, their velvety New Orleans Fizz. The rest of breakfast is traditional—eggs with excellent sausage or ham or bacon, served with hashed-and-browned potatoes. Everything is cooked to order, which accounts for much of the often-encountered waits, and the eggs are especially well prepared. The leisurely, mellow Irish Coffee conclusion will make this a breakfast you will long remember, if the mood captures you. And if it doesn't, what are you doing in our wonderful San Francisco anyhow?

I know it might be difficult to think of lunch and dinner right at this moment but in San Francisco, where reservations are required in almost all important restaurants, you have to do just that. My recommendations for lunch give you a choice of either a tiny inexpensive Chinatown spot, where you can savor delightful dim sum (Chinese luncheon tidbits) in an informal atmosphere; or else a feast for the eyes, if not exactly for the palate, in one of the world's most beautiful dining rooms, the Garden Court of the Palace Hotel. You might wish to read ahead for my full descriptions of these unique lunch spots before making up your mind. No reservations are accepted at the dim sum house, but if you opt for the Garden Court, you should call 392-8600 for a 12:30 p.m. reservation before you leave the Buena Vista.

For dinner, I offer three suggestions, giving you three vastly different cuisines in three different price ranges. The first is L'Etoile (771-1529; reservations imperative), the city's most chic French restaurant with a distinguished cuisine to match its elegant and very expensive ambience. My second: Square One (788-1110; reservations a must) is an exciting California-cuisine restaurant with what I consider upper moderate prices. And my third suggestion is Paprikas Fono (441-1223; reservations recommended) a moderately-priced restaurant in colorful Ghirardelli Square where, if you are lucky, you can enjoy a Bay view as well as excellent Hungarian fare. (Full reviews of these three restaurants are found later in this book. Of course, if you wish to try other restaurants, you will find a complete listing of my personal favorites in the special index in the back.) In addition to making these arrangements, if you are planning to drive the 49-Mile Drive yourself, you might wish to telephone your favorite rental car company to make certain they will have a car for you this afternoon at about 2:00 p.m. Once all these necessary phone calls are completed, you can start your walking tour of the Fisherman's Wharf area.

10:00 a.m.   When you leave the Buena Vista Cafe, turn left and walk one block down Beach Street. Here you will find Ghirardelli Square, a colorful shopping-dining complex created from an old chocolate factory. (You'll find more about Ghirardelli Square on Day Two.) Across the street is Aquatic Park and the Maritime Museum (open every day; 10:00 a.m. to 6 p.m.). If you have youngsters along, they'll be thrilled with the huge sea anchors and other ocean-going memorabilia on display at the museum; and be sure to show them the intricate miniature clipper ships and freighters. Older folks may want to drop in at the Senior Citizens' Center, located on the lower floor.

After leaving the museum, walk down onto the beach for a view of the Golden Gate Bridge—provided the fog is not in! On the beach, turn right, back toward the Victorian Park and down Jefferson Street. Just past the San Francisco Rowing Club, you will find the Hyde Street Pier (open daily; 10:00 a.m. to 5:00 p.m.; no admission charge). Docked here are five historic ships which you can explore with the aid of audio wands. These electronic devices enable you to hear pre-recorded stories of the ships, as well as wind and weather sound effects. After leaving the Hyde Street Pier, continue down Jefferson Street toward Fisherman's Wharf.

However, before arriving at the Wharf proper, you may wish to take a slight detour to The Cannery, a dramatic dining-shopping complex of unusual design. You can't miss it, for it is on the right-hand side of Jefferson Street as you approach Fisherman's Wharf.

If you are lucky enough to be here when the famous local San Francisco crabs are in season (usually mid-November to mid-May), you are in for a real treat. Crabs are served in San Francisco all year around but during the off-season, they come in iced from other areas. The famous San Francisco crab is not to be confused with the smaller, soft-shelled crab of the East Coast. It is closer in flavor and size to the eastern lobster rather than to the eastern crab. The best way to enjoy our marvelous crab is freshly picked from the shell, sprinkled with lemon juice or dipped into a plain, good-quality mayonnaise, perhaps flavored with a dash of mustard.

One of the few San Francisco culinary habits I do not endorse is covering crab with something called Louis sauce. I have never met Louis but I would gladly strangle him for his creation, which overpowers the crab's delicate flavor. Louis dressing, by the way, seems to be nothing but a diabolic mixture of mayonnaise and catsup. And while at it, I should also like to veto the widespread practice of placing so-called cocktail sauce on San Francisco crab. That's more destructive than Louis!

Another seafood delicacy which you will find at the Wharf is the "tiny bay shrimp." Many years ago, San Francisco Bay was filled with delectable little crustaceans very similar to these and thus the name "bay shrimp." However, man's pollution and the high cost of fishing for the few that remain in the Bay put an end to their being commercially fished locally. Therefore, just about all the "bay shrimp" you will find on the Wharf and in restaurants come from up and down the Pacific Coast and are shipped in iced.

By the way, since seafood terminology has never been universally standardized, most local restaurants reserve the term "shrimp" for these tiny crustaceans, and "prawns" for the larger ones. There are no local varieties of prawns; the vast majority of those you find in San Francisco are shipped in from the coast of Mexico or New Orleans, usually frozen. Oh, yes, while I strenuously object to the cocktail sauce on crab, I do enjoy it on shrimp. But even then I request it be served "on the side" in order that I may add just the right amount.

At this point, I might tell you about a feud I had with one of our famous local Italian restaurants. The owner insisted upon serving his shrimp cocktails with spoons rather than forks. When I objected, he told me there was too much sauce to use a fork. This, of course, was exactly my point! But plead as I might to use less sauce, he persisted and seems to be doing nicely without my patronage.

Your stroll along Fisherman's Wharf will also introduce you to another San Francisco culinary favorite—our famous sourdough bread. You will spot it either in a heavy, round dome or in a long, cylindrical baton like the traditional French bread loaf. The dome-like loaf has a very hard outer crust with a rather coarse texture inside; the long cylindrical loaf seems to have a softer crust and a smoother inner texture—both, of course, possess a slight sour taste. Natives continually complain that the sourdough isn't as sour as it once was, which may be true. Nevertheless, it is still one of the world's greatest breads. Oh, if you fall in love with our sourdough and wish to take a "bite" of San Francisco home with you, you will find racks of them at the airport. But we had better be moving on along the Wharf right now.

At the water's edge near Pier 43½, you will find your closest, land-based view of Alcatraz. If one of the world's most famous former prisons truly fascinates you (it holds no interest for me), you might want to visit the "Rock." However, reservations for your jaunt to Alcatraz Island, now part of the Golden Gate Recreation Area of the National Park Service, usually must be made in advance for a specific day and time. Sometimes, in the peak visitor season, there can be up to a three-week wait! Therefore, it is best to reserve tickets in advance through Ticketron, Inc. by calling 392-SHOW or visiting one of their outlets located in the Emporium on Market Street and in Tower and Rainbow Record Stores. (By the way, throughout this guide you will find that Ticketron is the best source for reservations for such diverse attractions as the Monterey Bay Aquarium, Hearst Castle, etc. I have always found them inordinately efficient.) Should you decide to go to Alcatraz at some time during your stay, be sure to wear warm clothing and sturdy walking shoes.

If you haven't seen enough ships at the Hyde Street Pier, your next stop should be further along the water-front at Pier 43 to board the Balclutha. But keep an eye on your watch; we have a full day planned.

The Balclutha is the last full-rigged ship of the great Cape Horn Fleet. It has been faithfully restored through the generosity of its sponsor, the San Francisco Maritime Museum Association, as well as through contributions from public-spirited San Franciscans, and by members of San Francisco unions who donated thousands of labor hours without charge. Your admission fee goes toward its upkeep.

Although the Balclutha is anchored permanently at Pier 43, it is easy to imagine her anchor is aweigh and you are sailing off in freedom and glory on the world's trade routes for the romantic past of the Balclutha hangs to her from stem to stern. Even the galley and captain's cabin have been restored accurately. If you have any youngsters in your party, looking over every part of this great ship will be certainly one of the highlights of your visit to San Francisco. And even if no children are present, who among us cannot be caught up in the magical day-dream of casting off in a full-rigged sailing ship like the Balclutha?

11:45 a.m. Walk three blocks up Taylor Street away from Fisherman's Wharf and you will find the terminal point of another cable car line, the Powell Street line. Board here.

If you have decided on the Chinese dim sum lunch, get off at Pacific Avenue and walk downhill to Tung Fong, 808 Pacific Avenue (362-7115; open for lunch every day except Wednesday). San Francisco has a vast assortment of dim sum restaurants, but this tiny hole-in-the-wall is regarded as one of the finest exponents of this intriguing Chinese luncheon tradition. While other huge dim sum emporiums, such as Asia Garden down the street and the Hong Kong across the street, may perhaps offer a greater variety of dishes, I give the edge on quality to little Tung Fong.

Dim sum, which translates as "heart's delights," are one of the great delights of Chinese cookery. They are little snacks which offer an exquisite array of textures and flavors. If you have never experienced a dim sum lunch, all you need to remember is to remain open-minded and adventuresome! There is no set menu: what you do is hail a tray-laden waitress and select at random any of the stuffed dumplings, tiny sparerib sections, egg rolls, custard tarts, or whatever else happens to be on the tray. You will then be served a small plate containing two or three portions of each selection. There are no prices; your check will be tabulated by adding up the empty plates at the end of the meal. But let yourself go. Prices are remarkably low and you can eat for hours for about $7.00 per person. Be sure to include favorites such as Chicken in Foil; Char Sil Bow (barbecued pork in a puffy steamed bun); Fon Gor (pink shrimp visible through the thin steamed-dough covering); and Custard Tart for your dessert—each sensational!

After your filling dim sum lunch, a walk through Chinatown before getting behind the wheel of your rented car or in the seat of a tour bus would feel just right. So proceed downhill to Grant Avenue, turn right, and you will find yourself in the heart of Chinatown—the world's largest Chinese community outside the Far East. You are taking your stroll at the best time of day, too, for this is when the streets are packed with Chinese residents doing their marketing for the evening meal. Because of the reliance of Chinese cuisine on the freshest ingredients, Chinese women shop daily in the afternoon. Thus, you will find the fish markets, delicatessens and green grocers jammed with shoppers—and I daresay you will be among them, for the aromas streaming out of Chinatown's markets are simply enticing! Street scenes in Hong Kong or Taipei are hardly more colorful or more fun!

Naturally, in between the food shops (the mainstay of Chinatown's residents) are the curio and gift stores. The quality of wares to be found here ranges from blatant junk to priceless antiques. During your Fourth Perfect Day, I will devote a whole morning to a walking tour of Chinatown, but right now it's just window-shopping and strolling as you head toward downtown San Francisco.

If you decided not to lunch at Tung Fong but rather at the elegant Garden Court—by elegant, I mean the dining room itself, not the food—then you can either get off the cable car at Pacific and take a pre-lunch walk through Chinatown along Grant Avenue to Market Street (about nine blocks) or, if you are a little weary of walking, simply stay on the cable car until it reaches Market Street. Here, get off and turn left toward the Ferry Building Tower (you will see it at the end of the street). Walk about four blocks and you will be at the Palace Hotel, Market at New Montgomery (392-8600; lunch served Monday through Friday; buffet brunch served on Sunday), with its breathtaking Garden Court.

The Garden Court was once one of the city's proudest dining rooms and the hotel itself was called "the world's grandest hotel" at its opening in 1875. Luckily, we still have the Garden Court (preserved as a historical monument) to remind us what hotel architecture was like in that era of gracious spaciousness before the invention of plastic and neon. And should you be extra lucky in lunching there on a sunny day with the sun's rays streaming through the high, glassed ceiling, breaking into rainbow hues as they hit the prisms of the huge chandeliers, you might believe you are really back in the year 1875.

If the opulent Garden Court has not changed much during this century, its cuisine has—and all for the worse! Yet, localite and visitor alike can still enjoy the magic of this room by skirting the more ambitious luncheon offerings and ordering the famous Palace Court Salad or the Green Goddess Salad. The Palace Court Salad consists of either shrimp, crab or chicken, bound with a judicious amount of mayonnaise, resting atop an artichoke bottom which stands on a tomato-slice base. Surrounding this are lettuce and chopped-egg mimosa. Served on the side is a sauce of Thousand Island Dressing.

"Green Goddess" was the name of a 1915 stage vehicle for actor George Arliss and it was the Palace's chef who invented this now nationally popular dressing as a tribute to the star. Over seventy years later, the kitchen is still turning out a commendable version of this mayonnaise-anchovy-tarragon blend (emphasis on the last ingredient) which dresses the lettuce topped with your choice of shrimp, chicken or crab in the Green Goddess Salad. The desserts, which may look tempting, are of coffee-shop accomplishment. But the room is what's memorable.

The Palace Hotel also has another room which you might enjoy seeing. The Pied Piper Room is right off the lobby near the Market street entrance. The claim to fame of this charming wood-panelled room is the huge Maxfield Parrish painting that spans the back of the bar.

2:00 p.m. Now it is time to see more of the city. Assuming that your one perfect day in San Francisco will not be too restrained by a budget, I have advised a rather expensive item for this afternoon—renting a car. My reason is the 49-Mile Drive. This driving-tour of the city is a magnificent concept, especially for San Francisco with its incredible views. And the people who conceived the idea certainly deserve the undying gratitude of residents and visitors alike.

The drive is very simple, even if you have never set foot inside the city's limits before, because the route is well marked. All along the 49-mile course are seemingly hundreds of blue-and-white seagull signs indicating the necessary turns and directions. Also, a complete map of the city with the drive clearly outlined is on sale at most bookstores and magazine stands, or available free of charge from the San Francisco Visitors & Convention

Bureau Information Center, located in Hallidie Plaza adjacent to the cable car turntable at the foot of Powell and Market Streets (open daily from 9 a.m., except Sundays from 10 a.m.). Because at times some of the 49-Mile Drive signs can be displaced due to road construction—or destroyed by vandals—I strongly recommend that you obtain this map before embarking on the drive. In addition, many of Golden Gate Park's roads are closed to automobile traffic on Sunday, and the Visitors Bureau map will show you an alternate route through the park. By the way, if you call the Visitors Bureau at a special number (391-2001), you will hear a recording of all important events in the city for that week.

Of course, if you would like to leave the driving to someone else, large comfortable chauffeur-driven limousines are available for less than what you might think from services such as Gray Line Limousine Service (885-8500). And if you cannot rent a car or limousine, do not feel disappointed in substituting the Gray Line Tour No. 1 of the city which leaves around 2:30 p.m. from their terminal at First and Mission Streets (771-4000). There will be a slight duplication on sights you have already seen this morning, such as Fisherman's Wharf, but certainly not enough to hamper your enjoyment. Since those taking either a limousine or the Gray Line Tour No. 1 will need no further assistance, I will now personally conduct the 49-Mile Drive. Just ask your car rental office how to find the Civic Center.

2:15 p.m.   Start on Van Ness Avenue at the City Hall with its dome towering 308 feet above the street—over 16 feet higher than the Capitol in Washington,D.C. Opposite it on Van Ness Avenue are twin buildings—the War Memorial Opera House and the Veteran's Building. Since its opening night performance on October 15, 1932 of *Tosca* with Muzio, the Opera House has been the hub of the city's cultural life and the home of the opera, symphony and ballet.

Across Grove Street is the newer Louise M. Davies Symphony Hall. Opened with a nationally televised concert in 1980, this is now the home of the San Francisco Symphony. Even though it is graced by a large Henry Moore sculpture, its curved glass facade is often likened to that of a giant bus terminal. And even nastier things are said about its problematic acoustics inside.

Next door to the Opera House is the Veteran's Building in which, on its upper floors, is the Museum of Modern Art with a permanent collection including Matisse, Picasso, Rivera, and others. However, now is not the time for museum-viewing—I've scheduled that later on in your stay. This afternoon, we just want to get a feeling of the entire city. So off you go up Van Ness Avenue, heading north.

At Geary Street, you will spot a 49-Mile Drive marker; turn left. Proceed along Geary, and in two blocks on your left you will see imposing St. Mary's Cathedral, seat of the Roman Catholic archdiocese of San Francisco. Soon you will pass the Japanese Trade & Cultural Center on the right. Here you exit Geary on the right at the 49-Mile Drive sign. But instead of turning sharp right, as the marker indicates, drive directly ahead one block to Fillmore Street—then turn right. (If you followed the 49-Mile Drive sign, it would direct you back downtown, through Chinatown and Fisherman's Wharf, which you have seen.) Continue out Fillmore Street. It soon plunges (use low gear) from the crest of Pacific Heights down to the Bay's edge. Here at Marina Boulevard, turn left for three blocks to Scott Street. Another left onto Scott places you back on the official 49-Mile Drive route, with its familiar blue-and-white seagull signs, leading you to the Palace of Fine Arts.

The Palace of Fine Arts, designed by Bernard Maybeck, derives its name from the role it played in the 1915 Panama-Pacific International Exposition when it housed the art exhibit. Today, it is the last remaining building of the Exposition. Several years ago, when the Palace was about to fall apart from old age, Walter Johnson of San Francisco donated over $2 million toward its restoration, with the city and state also contributing. Proponents of modern architecture suggested the money be used to tear down the building. San Franciscans were aghast at such an idea, having long treasured the Palace as a symbol of a past era when buildings were created as a feast for the eye rather than solutions to economic and functional needs.

Thus, the Palace of Fine Arts is today as it was yesterday—that is, in outward appearance. Inside, there is a 20th-century museum called Exploratorium. The theme is perception, and there are over 200 exhibits which you can manipulate and activate to make you more aware of your perceptional powers. The Exploratorium (563-3200) is open Wednesday 1:00 p.m. to 9:30 p.m.(no admission from 6:00 p.m.); Thursday and Friday from 1:00 p.m. to 5:00 p.m.; Saturday and Sunday from 10:00 a.m. to 5:00 p.m.; closed Monday and Tuesday.

Next, you enter the Presidio, the largest military reservation within a city's limits in the United States. The date—1776—on the gate as you enter is not a mistake because the Presidio served as military headquarters of the soldiers of Charles III of Spain in that year. Later, on your left, you will pass the Officers' Club which is the only, and therefore the oldest, remaining adobe building erected by the Spaniards in San Francisco. Throughout your drive in the Presidio, you will be favored by panoramic views of the Bay and the Golden Gate.

On your left, as you proceed, you will see the National Military Cemetery, significant in that no other cemetery lies within the city limits. Peter B. Kyne, an author, loved to tell the story of how the authorities dealt with his plan to be buried in this cemetery, because it was the only possible way he could be interred within the confines of the city he loved so much. Being a veteran, he went one day to chat with the Commanding Officer, to whom he confided his great desire. When he asked the Commanding Officer if he could reserve a plot, the latter merely glanced at Mr. Kyne and replied in gruff tones, "Mr. Kyne, first come, first served!"

After winding through the Presidio's tree-lined streets,

which always remind me of some sleepy college campus of years ago, you will begin climbing up toward the Golden Gate Bridge. However, watch for a sign on the right indicating Fort Point, where you will take a slight detour. Situated at the strategic entrance to San Francisco Bay, the massive brick and iron fort was constructed in 1853, using Fort Sumter as a rough model. Its huge structure is impressive and so are the views of the Bay, the city, and the underside of the Golden Gate Bridge which is high above you. Do not spend too much time snapping spectacular pictures, though, for there are many miles and equally impressive sights ahead. By the way, going at a fairly leisurely pace with several short stops, the 49-Mile Drive takes about four hours.

From Fort Point, retrace your route back up to the main road, turning right. An optional detour is a few yards beyond this turn which would take you to a parking area near the Golden Gate Bridge Toll Plaza. However, I suggest you press on and reserve that stop for a few days later when you go over the bridge.

Again, following the now familiar blue-and-white seagull signs, continue through the Presidio and on to Sea Cliff with its beautiful homes overlooking the entrance to the Bay.

Our drive takes us next to the Palace of the Legion of Honor, an art museum which also serves as a memorial to California's dead of the First World War. There are museums throughout the world with superior collections but few, if any, with a more magnificent setting. You will certainly want to park here and spend a few moments looking at both the Palace itself and the panoramic view it commands.

Returning to the 49-Mile Drive route and proceeding along Geary Boulevard, you will soon find the historic Cliff House on your right—and directly before you, the vast panorama of the Pacific Ocean pounding upon miles of beach. The site of the Cliff House has been the locale for a restaurant ever since 1863 because of its vantage point overlooking the beach and rocks below where sea lions make their home. However, the building which now stands there is certainly not the original. In fact, there have been many Cliff Houses—most of which have been lost to fires. One was even blasted from its foundations when, in 1887, a schooner loaded with 40 tons of dynamite was driven onto the bluff below and exploded. Looking far off to your right, if it is an exceptionally clear day, you will be able to see the Farallon Islands. San Francisco's city limits actually extend 32 miles west into the ocean to include this cluster of islands.

Now, on down the Great Highway, past Fleishhacker Zoo, circling Lake Merced and onto Sunset Boulevard (not to be confused with the neon-jungle street of Hollywood fame) to Golden Gate Park, turning right as you enter the park.

How can I characterize this stupendous municipal undertaking except to say that few cities in the world can claim a park within their limits as beautiful and natural, yet entirely man-made! Today, your 49-Mile Drive will take you along most of the park's main drives just to give you a perspective of its beauty and space. However, Golden Gate Park deserves far more than this cursory look and tomorrow, we will devote a whole afternoon to some of its delights, although it would actually take several days to fully explore its wonders. So just relax and enjoy your drive.

After exiting the park, turn right up Stanyan Street . . . then right onto Parnassus Avenue, passing the huge University of California Medical School campus. Then on to Twin Peaks. From its 910-foot summit, the panorama of San Francisco and the East Bay spreads before you. On a clear day, it is one of the most spectacular city views in the world; if it is foggy, you'll just have to buy a postcard of the view back at your hotel. As you drive down Twin Peaks Boulevard and Roosevelt Way, you will catch sight of every conceivable type of architecture in this popular view-conscious neighborhood. Many of the houses perch high atop stilt-like foundations, craning over the roofs of others for a better view.

Crossing Market Street, your next stop is Mission Dolores, founded by the Franciscan Fathers in 1776 with the historic church dating from 1782. After your visit to Mission Dolores, continue on up Dolores Street. Here you will see a wild assortment of San Franciscan Victorian houses. Some years ago it became the vogue to restore these lovely old residences, but I feel many have gone too far in the use of color, often picking out the ornate wood details in rainbow hues. Nevertheless, they are great fun to see and some are very handsome. Eventually, a left turn onto Army Street will take you into the industrial section of the city and onto one of the freeway routes (Highway 280) back towards downtown.

From elevated Highway 280, you will see spread before you the skyline of downtown San Francisco. It provides quite a grand finale for your tour. Leave the freeway at Fourth Street, and again following the familiar 49-Mile Drive signs, you will soon pass along San Francisco's once-bustling Embarcadero waterfront and historic Ferry Building.

One of the biggest blights on the city's beauty is the overhead freeway above you, which gives a depressing feeling to what could be an inordinately beautiful waterfront. As we go to press, a new movement is afoot to tear down this civic blunder; however, if the freeway still looms over your head as you drive past the Ferry Building, the efforts obviously have not succeeded.

Opposite the Ferry Building is a fine bricked and planted plaza with one of the town's most controversial landmarks, the Vaillancourt walk-thru fountain. Many hailed its construction as the ultimate in modern design, while others have derided its appearance as something left by a dog with square bowels. You be your own judge! Your route now takes you through the financial district and onto Market Street, where the 49-Mile Drive ends. Find the shortest route back to your hotel for a brief rest and freshening up before hitting the town again for cocktails.

7:00 p.m. To watch it grow dark from the Top of the Mark has been a favorite San Francisco twilight pastime ever since the Mark Hopkins Hotel was built on its choice Nob Hill site. By this time, you should know where the Mark Hopkins Hotel is—you passed within a half block of it this morning on your cable car ride. Even though a dozen skyscraper hotels and office buildings now boast view restaurants and cocktail lounges on their uppermost floor, top honors still go to the Top of the Mark.

Before you select a table, do not hesitate to walk around the room, sampling the 360-degree view of America's most beautiful city. My perennial choice of table is on the west side (to the right as you enter the room) facing the Golden Gate and the setting sun. The Top of the Mark is always crowded and a prime table may be difficult to find; however, you can enjoy some aspects of the view from almost any table.

8:00 p.m.   Leave the Mark Hopkins, cross California Street and enter the Hotel Fairmont, which boasts what is probably America's most famous hotel lobby since it is featured in the TV hit series, *Hotel*. Our Fairmont is TV's St. Gregory. Here you may wish to stop for another cocktail or simply stroll around.

The Fairmont was designed by the famous architect, Stanford White, and rebuilt in 1907 after the fire had almost completely destroyed the original structure. (You will note here that San Franciscans prefer to refer to the 1906 tragedy as "the fire" rather than the earthquake. This is to make it clear that most of the damage was done by the ensuing fire rather than by the earthquake itself.)

Leaving the Fairmont, you will see the famous Pacific Union Club across the street. The club's great contribution to San Francisco lies in preserving the only remaining famous Nob Hill mansion, built in 1885 at a cost of over $1.5 million by James Flood who was one of the Bonanza Barons. Today, it stands as a fortress of Republicanism.

Walking past the Flood Mansion and Huntington Park, just across Taylor Street, you will find the imposing and splendid Grace Cathedral. The site, contributed by the famous Crocker family, was once the location of their mansion. The Cathedral houses the first seat of the Protestant Episcopal Church in America.

If the days are long enough, you may wish to wander around the crest of Nob Hill where you will see breathtaking views in almost every direction. The Masonic Temple is here, too, with its surprising wall of "glass" which you can see by peering through the front doors. Although it looks like a huge stained-glass window, the wall is actually a mosaic fused between two sheets of transparent plastic.

8:30 p.m.   Selecting where to dine on the first evening in any strange city is always a major decision for me. And reaching my choice of recommendations for you has involved a great deal of soul, as well as palate, searching. This was not true when the first edition of this guide appeared some twenty-five years ago. At that time, there was no doubt your first dinner should be at Trader Vic's. The Trader Vic restaurant empire was launched right across the Bay in Oakland. But once the San Francisco "branch" was established at 20 Cosmo Place (776-2232; dinner served nightly), it became the crown jewel, probably because Vic himself was in residence there. And not only was the food of topnotch quality, but a special room, the Captain's Cabin, soon became the social sanctum sanctorum of the city's elite.

But as the years passed, the cuisine began to develop some flaws, especially when served outside "the Cabin." Therefore, today I can no longer unequivocally recommend my old favorite Trader Vic's to the "unknown" visitor. However, if you happen to be a celebrity of any name recognition or if you have local friends who are "Cabin regulars" and can guarantee you entry into this vastly enjoyable room, dinner at Trader Vic's can still be a memorable experience. (Queen Elizabeth II, on her visit here in 1983, dined in a private room at Vic's in a very rare restaurant visit.) Yet, even in the Cabin I would restrict my ordering to the simpler, unsauced dishes (particularly those from the Chinese oven) and avoid the more ambitious preparations. Also in the Cabin, I strongly recommend you request the assistance of one of the captains in ordering. They are among the finest in town, thoroughly versed in the kitchen's output and on exactly how to pamper the most pampered international celebrities and local luminaries. Oh yes, don't be bashful in ordering one of Vic's justifiably famous rum concoctions—even the natives do!

If you are seriously interested in cuisine and are looking for the best, here are three different restaurants, ranging from very expensive to quite moderate, from which to choose for your first evening of San Francisco dining.

Although I steadfastly refuse to name any one San Francisco restaurant as the best, I have no reluctance to dub L'Etoile, 1075 California Street (771-1529; dinners nightly except Sundays; reservations imperative), the most chic. From the moment you step into its lengthy foyer and descend the sweeping staircase, you know you have entered a special place. The interior is inspired, the creation of Michael Taylor, one of the city's most renowned decorators. The scale of the room, the profusion of flowers held in gigantic urns, and the lighting's roseate glow create a gentle splendor evocative of Europe's most exalted dining salons. And, more importantly, L'Etoile's cuisine is very, very fine French.

For a first course, the Paillard of Salmon is exquisite. The wafer-thin slice of delicately pink salmon is poached to perfection and enrobed in a deft herb-butter sauce. Atop the salmon is a dollop of golden caviar, while stationed on the side is a thimble of ideally cooked angelhair pasta, moistened with a light cream sauce. A memorable dish. The truffle-freckled fish quenelles are also well handled, and their lobster sauce distinguished.

Throughout this guide, you will find me favoring lamb as a main course. This is primarily out of habit, not necessarily preference. You see, until not too long ago, veal on the West Coast was miserable, often bordering on baby beef. And our Western beef never has matched its mid-Western or Eastern cousins for flavor or tenderness. But our Western lamb is as fine as any in the world.

Therefore, lamb became my chosen meat. Today, with beautiful Mid-Western milk-fed veal available in our finer restaurants, I no longer have to be so restrictive. But old habits die hard. Yet, when the lamb is of L'Etoile's peerless quality, treated so understandingly (blushingly pink) their Rack of Lamb is impossible to resist. Scented with the herbs of Provence, this is lamb at its finest.

However, as I said, pristine white veal is now available and L'Etoile shows that this meat often requires a flavor enhancer to make it dazzle and their tangy mustard sauce does just that! Served with the veal are some superb sauteed wild mushrooms. A bevy of beautifully prepared vegetables—such as tomato-stuffed zucchini, baby carrots, etc.—adds color and flavor to each entree.

For dessert, their Souffle Grand Marnier is usually a winner; while their melange of desserts—a fragile fresh-fruit tartlet, a soupcon of one of their delicious made-on-the-premises sherbets, a mini frozen souffle—is ideal for those who want it all!

As a fitting grand finale, I would order a cafe filtre and a snifter of fine cognac, but ask that they be served in the bar. There, if Peter Mintun is at the keyboard, you will be soothed by the finest piano artistry to be heard this side of the Opera House stage!

While I would certainly not claim that L'Etoile serves the finest French cuisine in San Francisco (not with Le Castel, Pierre, and Sutter 500 in town!), it nevertheless combines award-winning performances by its interior decorator, kitchen, dining room staff and pianist into a total dining experience which lives up to its name—*the star*. Very expensive.

Square One, 190 Pacific Avenue at Front Street (788-1110; dinner served Monday through Saturday; lunch served weekdays; reservations a must) is the creation of Joyce Goldstein, an alumna of Berkeley's famed Chez Panisse. The decor is not unlike a clean-lined corporate cafeteria—blonde woods, unfrilly table settings, open kitchen. There is no doubt in anyone's mind that at Square One the food is the thing.

The daily-changing menu is an exciting eclectic gathering of worldwide dishes, often touched with the owner-chef's personal genius and daring. It's a style which can perhaps fall under the category 'California Cuisine', yet without the intrusion of what I call 'Dartboard Cooking.'

Dartboard Cooking describes for me the output of some trendy San Francisco kitchens, where obviously a blindfolded chef tosses several darts at a giant list of every imaginable ingredient. Where they hit is what he combines into dishes that have no rhyme nor reason. But at Square One there is the reason of a thoroughly knowledgeable chef who innately senses the congenialty of various foods and with them creates not rhyme but sheer poetry.

For example, for starters you might find a fresh pasta combined with red onion rings, slices of pancetta, slivers of sun-dried tomatoes, all of which have been lightly sauteed and then sprinkled with julienned raw basil leaves. Or if Ms. Goldstein is in a Morrocan mood, three North African salads—one of cumin-scented thinly sliced carrots, the other of eggplant and a third of slightly underdone lentils, aromatic with mint. Or Pasta e Fagioli, an Italian combination of shell pasta, white beans, flavored with pancetta and sunny with fresh tomatoes. Superb made-on-the-premises breads are ideal for sopping, dipping or just savoring with slabs of sweet butter.

While any chef can miscalculate, Ms. Goldstein seems incapable of error when it comes to dealing with pork. Her Roast Pork Florentine style, perfumed with rosemary, garlic and cloves is moist and tender. These two qualities, so elusive in many pork dishes, also are hallmarks in the pork loin treated to an orange-ginger glaze. Her Breast of Chicken Milanese presents a lightly-breaded succulent chicken breast touched with a lemon-caper sauce. Vegetables, of course, are always garden-fresh and superbly handled, such as grilled baby zucchini. Only once did the California cuisine penchant for too underdone vegetables rear its unwelcomed head with tiny new potatoes that could have used two more minutes of roasting.

For dessert, a Chocolate-Pecan torte is feather weight and refreshingly semi-sweet; its moistening moat a maple-flavored creme anglaise. The summertime Peach Pie is down-home perfection, especially when served with home-made ice cream. The wine list reflects the same care and understanding that makes Square One one of the city's finest restaurants. Upper-moderate price scale.

Paprikas Fono, Ghirardelli Square (441-1223; open every day for lunch and dinner; reservations advised), is a small piece of Hungary transplanted to the third floor of the square's Cocoa Building. Mr. and Mrs. Fono have not only accurately re-created the food of their native land but the delightful spirit and decor of a Hungarian inn, as well.

Naturally, you cannot pass up the native dish, Gulyas— a boldly red soup, thick with cubes of beef and potato, sprightly seasoned with paprika. Order some Langos with it and show your gastronomic savvy by rubbing these unsweetened crullers with raw garlic. As a main course, the Chicken Paprikas is succulent boned chicken breasts in a satiny paprika sauce served with the classic galuska, mini-dumplings similar to Swiss spaetzle. In contrast, the Casino Supper proves the Hungarian superiority in frying chicken. There are all sorts of tempting side dishes: Fresh Beet Salad and the ubiquitous Hungarian Cucumber Salad.

But you cannot leave Paprikas Fono without having some dessert, so save room. And for dessert, try Walnut Palacsintas to discover what Hungarian crepes are all about. Stuffed with pureed walnuts, these delectable pancakes are bathed in an ebony chocolate sauce. Wow! Or try Paulette's Torta, an almost sour chocolate cake of devastating richness. For a wine, there is Hungary's Egri Bikaver, bull's blood. And for an after-dinner drink, try a glass of sweet Hungarian Tokai to toast your first night in San Francisco.

If you can obtain a table in the glassed-in balcony, you

will have an exciting view of the Bay as background for an excellent yet moderately priced dinner. Truly a bargain.

11:00 p.m.   There is always a lot to do in San Francisco at this hour. But since nightclubs, comedy clubs, discos, jazz joints, etc. come and go so rapidly, I have never found it feasible to list them in these pages. But you can easily find out what is happening by consulting what everyone refers to as the "pink section"—that's its color, not its political leaning!—of San Francisco's only Sunday newspaper, *The Examiner-Chronicle*.

One nightclub which has survived for over forty years is the internationally famous Finocchio's. Finocchio's presented "drag" shows long before the word came into vogue. (Its more genteel translation is "female impersonators.") The lavishly costumed entertainers put on a tongue-in-cheek show which would hardly shock your maiden aunt from Oshkosh. But if you do visit this San Francisco landmark, be prepared to find busloads of conventioneers in the audience.

In San Francisco, "name" entertainment always plays the Venetian Room of the Fairmont Hotel. Joel Grey, our own Carol Channing, Tony "Left-My-Heart-Here" Bennett and other friends make annual visits. And there is usually a late show at about this hour.

2:00 a.m.   After the first edition of this guidebook appeared many years ago, my telephone rang about 2:05 a.m. The voice on the other end was that of an obviously inebriated woman. "Hi there," she slurred. "I love your guidebook and have been following your suggestions all day. But it's now two in the morning, all the places have closed and you have no more suggestions. What should I do?" I told her as gently as I could to go to bed, and the next day my phone number became unlisted.

However, for those of you still up, I have a couple suggestions. True, San Francisco, even with its overblown wicked reputation, does close up pretty tight at 2:00 a.m., the official "last call for alcohol" hour. Years ago, there were all sorts of places you could go to hear great jazz and drink watered-down scotch out of cracked coffee cups. But they are all gone—or at least that's what my cabbie-spies tell me. And even if they weren't, I couldn't recommend them in print—otherwise they would be gone for sure! So, how about taking a cab, or the car if you have it, and driving up Telegraph Hill to Coit Tower— the remarkable edifice fashioned after a fire hose nozzle as a tribute to our fire fighters by Lillie Hitchcock Coit— for a good-night look at the lights of San Francisco below you.

If you are hungry again, you can go to a jook house: Sam Wo Company, 813 Washington Street off Grant Avenue (open until 3:00 a.m.; closed Sunday). "Jook" is a type of Chinese rice gruel, served so piping hot that when you drop in your choice of raw beef, chicken, shrimp, fish, etc., it cooks almost instantly. My favorite is the one with fish; be sure to order a Chinese Doughnut with your gruel. I also enjoy their delicious Raw Fish Salad, Won Ton soup, and Beef-Tomato Soft Noodle Chow Mein. Sam Wo absolutely abounds in local color! Very inexpensive.

3:00 a.m. Good Night!

Now, if your plans provide for a longer stay in San Francisco, I shall take you through the second day of your one perfect week.

If not, you are now wiring your boss, explaining that this is the greatest city you have ever seen, and you simply have to stay for the rest of the week or month. (The author assumes no responsibility for the reply!)

So, read on to begin your Second Perfect Day.

Your Second Perfect Day Schedule

9:00 a.m. Breakfast at Sears'.

10:00 a.m. Shopping tour of downtown San Francisco.

12:00 noon Lunch at either Plum right off Union Square or at Greens with its Golden Gate view.

1:00 p.m. Drive or take easily accessible public transportation out to Golden Gate Park. See the Flower Conservatory, de Young Museum, the Asian Art Museum, the Aquarium and Planetarium, or just stroll.

4:00 p.m. Tea at the Japanese Garden.

4:30 p.m. Climb Strawberry Hill or feed the birds on the edge of Stow Lake.

5:00 p.m. Back to your hotel to freshen up for dinner.

6:30 p.m. Browse through Ghirardelli Square.

8:00 p.m. Dinner at Ghirardelli Square, either at the city's most renowned pan-China palace or at a colorful Italian restaurant, or enjoy fine French cuisine in a nearby elegant bistro.

10:00 p.m. A nightcap at the Buena Vista right down the street? Or just to bed . . . it's been a long day!

The Second Day of Your

One Perfect Week in San Francisco

9:00 a.m. There are many world travelers who will rush to Sears' at 439 Powell Street near Post (986-1160; closed Monday and Tuesday) for their first breakfast during each San Francisco stay, as quickly as others rush to the Top of the Mark for cocktails. Little wonder, for where in the world will you find your plate shimmering with 18 pancakes (small, thank goodness) crowned with whipped butter and maple syrup? And along with them, you can order excellent ham, bacon, link sausages or the very special Smoked Country Sausage patties made especially for Sears'.

Breakfast to many (and possibly this includes you) is the most important meal of the day. Sears' meets the challenge with distinction. Begin with an all-fresh Fruit Bowl instead of the traditional orange juice which, even here, is frozen. Then proceed to the famous pancakes; or to eggs beautifully cooked accompanied with crispy hash browns; or to a distinctive French toast made from San Francisco's famous sourdough bread. Then split an order of their baked-on-the-premises Coffee Cake. Closed for dinner but fine lunches are served until 2:30 p.m. Wednesday through Sunday.

10:00 a.m. You now find yourself in a perfect strategic position for a morning of shopping, serious or "window" variety. Whether you want to look for some personal needs which you neglected to pack, gifts for those back home or possibly for your host and hostess in San Francisco, or just splurge on yourself, Union Square is the place to start. Simply turn right for a half block when you exit Sears' and you are at Post Street, the northern boundary of the square. Cross Powell Street and you stand at the entrance of our first stop, Saks Fifth Avenue.

Saks Fifth Avenue: Opened in 1981, the interior is a masterpiece of design. Built around a central light well, criss-crossed by escalators, the store gives the shopper a feeling of openness and ease. Of course, the main attraction is the high-style merchandise, but I love the place just for its beautiful, elegant self.

Bullock and Jones: Facing Union Square further down Post Street is this handsome building, reminiscent of fine old British establishments devoted exclusively to apparel for the older man or the conservative younger one. They have a superb collection of fine English shoes and a Burberry's of London section on the third floor. Exiting Bullock and Jones, turn left down Post to Stockton, turning left again to inspect the charming Ruth Asawa fountain on the steps of the Hyatt On-Union-Square Hotel with its intricate details of San Francisco scenes.

The Tailored Man: At 324 Stockton, directly across from the Hyatt Hotel. In sharp contrast to nearby Bullock and Jones, this lively shop features at surprisingly reasonable prices the very latest men's styles, greatly influenced by European high fashions. And if you cannot find what you want, expert craftsmen will make a custom-tailored suit for you from a wide selection of imported fabrics.

Scheuer Linens: Immediately next door to the Tailored Man is this long-established and reliable shop. This is where countless San Francisco families obtain luxurious linens for dining room, bath and bedroom. Many imported items are available here and nowhere else.

Wedgwood San Francisco: Drop in here for the fine china to place upon those exquisite Scheuer linens.

Alfred Dunhill, Ltd.:   On the corner of Post and Stockton is the formidable local branch of this world-wide purveyor of cigars, pipe tobacco and leather goods, along with a small selection of men's clothes. (NOTE: For the pipe devotee, many visitors to San Francisco swear by the mixture sold by mail throughout the world at the Jim Mate Pipe & Tobacco Shop, 575 Geary, 775-6634.)

Gumps: Just a few doors further down Post Street from Alfred Dunhill's you will find what is probably San Francisco's most internationally known shop, and for good reason. Although its early reputation was gained by its priceless jade collection and some of its merchandise is still on the expensive side, it has introduced many items of good taste at amazingly reasonable prices. It is one of the best gift shops in San Francisco and certainly a place which deserves your attention if you plan to take gifts home as a reminder of your trip. You can browse through Gump's at your leisure, and you should not miss the jade collection on the third floor, or the limited but fine collection of lithographs and paintings. Gump's also offers a topnotch framing service.

Elizabeth Arden: Should any women visitors require "touch-up's" during their stay, this branch of the international chain is conveniently found in between Gump's and Eddie Bauer.

Eddie Bauer: Famed for its goose-down products—from outdoor wear to indoor comforters—this store also carries men and women's sportswear, as well as everything you need for that camping or fishing expedition.

Shreve's: Corner of Post and Grant. The Tiffany of the West Coast, or perhaps it is true, as some San Franciscans maintain, that Tiffany's is the Shreve's of the East Coast. Either way, this is for you if you love the beautiful in china, sterling and jewelry. Now let us cross Grant Avenue and turn left for one block.

Don Sherwood Golf & Tennis World: At the corner of Grant and Sutter is this 8,500 square-foot emporium stocked with just about anything the athlete desires.

Tiffany's: A very small version of the New York original, but you can easily spend just as much money.

Banana Republic Travel and Safari Clothes: If you are actually going off to some exotic land or just like the loose, super-casual look of safari clothes, you will want to pass through the elephant-tusk archway.

Malm Luggage: The leading luggage and leather goods shop. Always on hand is one of the widest selections of functional, as well as beautiful, French Luggage made in California and sold in the nation's luxury stores. Malm also maintains a fine repair service, to which they can direct you in case of need.

Candy Jar: A must for chocoholics who may need a quick fix.

Tom Wing & Son: On the corner of Post and Grant is this fine purveyor of jade and oriental art objects.

A. Sulka & Co.; FAO Schwarz; Mark Cross: Next door to Tom Wing on Post Street, you will find this miniature reproduction of New York's Fifth Avenue.

Polo/Ralph Lauren: Further down the street, on the corner of Post and Kearny, is an entire shop devoted to one of the biggest names in American men's fashion. Frankly, I've always preferred Levis to designer jeans.

The Galleria at Crocker Center: Here is a mini-mall, three stories high, all covered over with a glass roof, which makes it ideal for rainy day strolling. Its wares are international in range—from Italy the trendy fashions of chic Gianni Versace; from England the fine shoes of Church's and the soaps and scents of Crabtree & Evelyn; from Belgium Godiva Chocolates. And don't overlook Card-o-logy, a small shop specializing in amusing and often risque greeting cards.

Now retrace your steps back up Post Street to Grant.

Brooks Brothers: On the southwest corner is the local branch of that staid old New York institution. Brooks' windows, which look as if they have not been changed since 1818, give many devotees a warm feeling that old values never die.

But instead of continuing on back up Post Street, turn down Grant Avenue toward Market Street.

Paul Bauer: Joined the street in 1982, displaying the finest in china and crystal, many with German accents.

Exclusive Cutlery Shop: A long-time San Francisco establishment specializing in knives, scissors and anything and everything that cuts.

Crate and Barrel: Directly across Grant Avenue is a colorful upscale version of a Cost Plus Imports with housewares from all over the globe.

Now you can head up Maiden Lane toward Union Square, where on the right hand side of the lane you will find . . .

Cartier: This is the back door, but it still leads you into one of the most famous jewelry stores around.

Edward Robison Co.:   Right across the lane from Cartier you will find frisky puppies, canaries and even perhaps a monkey or two. Many, many years ago, the Robison family owned a foodstore near the waterfront. Sailors, who in those long-ago days were usually deprived of fresh food on their lengthy sea voyages, often came in and bartered exotic birds and other pets for fresh edibles. Soon, the Robisons saw more potential in parakeets than in groceries. Thus today, many generations later, Edward Robison Co. remains the town's leading pet shop.

Circle Gallery: Number 140 is definitely the most famous building in the lane. This brown brick structure with its small, tunnel-like entrance is the only store in San Francisco, and one of the few in the world, designed by Frank Lloyd Wright. Here in 1949 he used the same architectural principle—a circular ramp—which he later used in his design for the Guggenheim Museum in New York. It provides an ideal setting for the gallery's handsome paintings.

Gucci: Next door to the Circle Gallery is the back door of *the* shop for those with the initial "G" or for those who do not mind carrying the designer's advertising all over their luggage, scarves and shoes.

Continuing up Maiden Lane, you reach Union Square.

San Francisco Ticket Box Office: In Union Square directly opposite Maiden Lane, offers half-price, day-of-performance tickets to many shows. It also houses a Bass Ticket outlet, which provides tickets for a wide variety of events.

Now turn left and walk a half block down Stockton Street to Geary.

Neiman-Marcus: For years it appeared as though the famed Texas institution would never come to Union Square. The site had been occupied for a century by the venerable City of Paris Department Store. When it ceased to be, there was a considerable movement to preserve the ancient building, primarily because of its huge rotunda, in which a giant Christmas tree was erected every December. Well, after endless law suits and delays, they finally obtained permission to demolish the building providing they would somehow incorporate the revered rotunda into the new building. That they did. And here it is, a part of old San Francisco in the newest addition to Union Square. Now if they would only do something about the ugly harlequin pattern on the facade! (By the way, on its upper level the restored rotunda now houses a restaurant of the same name. And while the place is physically delightful, situated directly under the huge, multi-colored 26,000-piece glass dome, the cuisine is problematic.)

I. Magnin and Company: Even with the arrival of Saks (1981) and Neiman-Marcus (1982) to Union Square, I. Magnin still reigns as the *grande dame* to San Franciscans. Its clean, white, elegant exterior is matched by the elegance within. But don't let its austerity put you off. Even those on a very limited budget can find many items in excellent taste. And although noted mostly as a women's apparel shop, its men's department and gourmet food section are well worth investigating.

Macy's: As an overall department store, Macy's is with-out any doubt the most popular in downtown San Francisco. Not only does it literally surround I. Magnin, but has even extended across Stockton Street, housing its enormous men's and children's departments in a building next to Neiman-Marcus. At Macy's there is something for everyone and at every price.

By now, you are probably beat. And we have a long afternoon of walking ahead. So we will end our shopping tour of Union Square here and decide on lunch. But before we do, let me give you a few more stores in the vicinity, which you may wish to check out on your own later in your stay.

The Emporium: Market Street, between Fourth and Fifth. Aptly named, this is reputedly the largest single store in Northern California. It is a true department store in the grand manner.

Woolworth's: Yes, Woolworth's. But this is one of the country's largest, and actually it is more than a store—it's a carnival! Here you will see orchids and pizzas sold a few steps from each other. And the din will be aug-mented by the shouts of a demonstrator, hawking the latest gadget designed to revolutionize your life. There is even a fancy food department with such rarities as canned buffalo meat and genuine Swedish hardtack. You'll find Woolworth's on the corner of Market and Powell Streets, directly opposite the Emporium.

Anthony's Shoe Repairing Shop: 54 Geary Street. Not only is this little shop known for top quality shoe and handbag repairing while you wait, but also for its out-standing shoe-dye facilities. They will even mail their work anywhere in the country.

For years, the 400 block of Post Street was *the* shopping street in the Union Square area. But then Sutter Street, which is parallel to Post, one block north, began attract-ing some extremely interesting shops

Wilkes Bashford, Ltd.:   336 Sutter Street. That Mercedes stretch limo double-parked in front is probably that of the current rock-star rage, loading up on some of the town's trendiest threads. Here are some of tomorrow's fashions, which can be as mind-boggling as their price tags. You'll find the women's department directly across the street. (NOTE: As we go to press the fate of Wilkes Bashford at this location is uncertain. After a scandal involving questionably low rent payments to the city, which owns the building, Bashford may be evicted and forced to relocate.)

Two blocks up from Bashford's, there is a whole enclave of superb shops.

Pierre Deux: 532 Sutter. Here is a trove of treasures if you are decorating your maison in the French Provincial manner.

Therien & Company: 534 Sutter. Leave Pierre Deux with some cash to spare and you can walk directly into this beautiful antique shop without even stepping on the sidewalk.

Saint Laurent Rive Gauche: 540 Sutter. Located on the right-hand side of the street, St. Laurent's Left Bank boutique offers high French fashion.

The Forgotten Woman: 550 Sutter. Just because a lady cannot slip into St. Laurent's slinkier numbers, there is no reason she should be forgotten in the world of fashion. And in this special shop she is not—in fact, here she reigns supreme!

Laura Ashley: 563 Sutter. Here you will find those lovely floral Ashley fabrics in dresses or in home design.

Jeffrey Davies: 575 Sutter. I generally detest artificial flowers, but the silk beauties you will find here are breathtaking. Often customers smell them to make certain they are not real. Fantastic arrangements are shipped anywhere. An intriguing shop not to be missed.

Williams-Sonoma: 576 Sutter Street. This is the mother store for what has become a national chain of culinary shops. Inside you will discover just about anything you can imagine—and even some things you can't—for the preparation and serving of food. Ask if they will be having any of their cooking demonstrations during your stay; admission is free, and famous cooking instructors and authors are guest teachers. Also, you might wish to ask that your name be placed on their mailing list to receive their excellent catalogue.

12:00 noon.   After a morning of shopping, it would be wise for you to lunch downtown so you will be fairly close to your hotel, to which you can return for a rest prior to our afternoon activities in Golden Gate Park. This day, as with most days of properly seeing any city, involves a considerable amount of "on your feet" activity. Thus, midday rests are good investments for maximum enjoyment.

If your memories of restaurants in department stores are none too happy, little wonder. For all too many years, these eateries have set forth shop-worn chicken salads, as if women would not accept anything more substantial. But today, things are looking up. And in the basement of Macy's men's store, O'Farrell at Stockton, you will find a pleasantly creative place simply called Plum (984-7463; lunch served daily except Sunday).

Although an adjacent stylish cafeteria shares some of the menu items at slightly lower prices, the attractive aura of Plum more than compensates for the nominal increase. Panels covered with photographs of old San Francisco break up the large space into more intimate and comfortable sections, while rich browns and natural woods mitigate any possible sterile feeling and provide a restful oasis from the shopping area bustle. Soups tend to be topnotch while omelettes and salads are distinctively delicious. In the latter category, there are two outstanding attractions—a rarely found, truly authentic Salade Nicoise; and an even more unusual Chilled Julienne of Beef. Among the outstanding hot dishes are calf's liver served with avocado (a seemingly incompatible marriage which ends very happily); beef bourguignonne; and stuffed eggplant. The dessert cart holds some superb chocolate cakes and fruit tarts. Your choice of several teas or cafe filtre concludes a pleasantly restful lunch. Typical Plum touches such as their use of sweet butter and unusually fine French baguettes, give this charming room a decidedly European flair. Oh yes, Plum can become quite crowded at lunchtime; a line usually forms at about noon. However, you can bypass it, if you call ahead for reservations. Moderate.

My alternate luncheon recommendation is best reached by car. And because it is so enormously popular, reservations here are a must—and they should be made as far in advance as possible. Failing to obtain a reservation, you can probably be seated without much of a wait (but in a rather uncomfortable quasi-cocktail area), if you arrive promptly when the doors open at 11:30 a.m. Are all these complications worth the effort? Yes! Because Greens is one of San Francisco's most unusual and exciting restaurants.

Greens, Building A, Fort Mason (771-6222; lunch served Tuesday through Saturday) is situated in a barn-like structure, formerly a warehouse in what was an army fort. The barrenness of the massive, high-ceilinged room makes for a rather high noise level. But there are compensations: one wall of windows affords a magnificent view of the Marina, Golden Gate and Marin headlands, provided the fog is not in!

Begin with one of the Greens' soups, regardless of what it is. The kitchen appears nigh infallible in conjuring up creations such as a velvety Eggplant Soup, enlivened by a soupcon of garlicky rouille. And even if you are on the strictest diet, don't dare miss out on Greens' sensational house-baked breads. Greens is owned and operated by The Zen Center, which also runs one of the city's finest bakeries, Tassajara, the provider of Greens' baked goods. The basket on your table will usually include three different varieties. Hopefully it will contain a peerless egg twist or their French country rye, a monumental bread.

For a main course, Greens usually offers a pasta dish,

such as ideally al dente fettucine tossed with brocolli flowerettes, sun-dried tomatoes, pinenuts, olive oil, fresh herbs and plenty of garlic. Or try something like their Tostados—corn tortillas with refried blackbean chili, guacamole, jack cheese, lettuce, tomatoes, creme fraiche and cilantro. It is served with a hauntingly zesty salsa piquante. A Gruyere Cumin Tart was perfectly baked with a sauteed leek-and-cheese filling. And, if possible, try to have one of their salads, the greens of which probably were grown on the Zen Center's organic farm, Green Gulch, in Marin County.

But forgo a salad if it will interfere with your having a dessert, again from Tassajara's ovens. It might be the perfect Pumpkin Pie, a Boysenberry-Raspberry Tart with a melt-in-your-mouth crust, or a luscious Banana-Walnut cake. Greens serves no hard liquor, but always presents a limited but select offering of some of California's most interesting wines, available either by the glass or bottle.

Oh, by the way, perhaps you did not notice it but the above recommended lucullan lunch contained not a speck of meat, fowl or fish. You see, Greens is strictly vegetarian. And that makes it all the more remarkable. In terms of culinary acumen, I consider Greens' kitchen to be one of the finest in the city. And when you consider that they work within the restricting confines of unbreachable vegetarian rules, their virtuosity becomes all the more astonishing. Because of their wondrous ways with flavors and textures, I somehow never notice that my meal at Greens lacks meat and/or fish. And that is the highest compliment I can pay them!

If you can't fit Greens in today—or it can't fit you in!—reserve for later in the week. But don't miss it. (To reach Greens from downtown, drive out to Van Ness Avenue, turn right to Bay Street, left on Bay to Laguna, and right on Laguna to Marina Blvd. The entrance to the Fort Mason Center, where Greens is located, is at Marina Blvd. and Buchanan.)

1:00 p.m. And now for an afternoon in the park—San Francisco's inimitable Golden Gate Park. The park can be easily reached by public transportation or by car. The only necessity one must take is comfortable shoes, since seeing and feeling the beauty of the park is best experienced on foot.

For those driving from Greens, turn right onto Marina Blvd. after exiting the fort. Continue along Marina for about five blocks to Divisadero Street, then left onto Divisadero. Divisadero will take you over the crest of Pacific Heights and through the Western Addition to Fell Street. Turn right on Fell, first bearing to the left and then to the right as you enter the park proper. This places you on John F. Kennedy Drive and, in a few seconds, you will come to our first stop, the Flower Conservatory which is on your right.

Now, let me allow those of you who had lunch downtown and are coming by bus to catch up. To reach Golden Gate Park by bus, simply walk down Stockton Street to Market. Board either a Hayes #21 or Fulton #5 bus which will eventually take you along Fulton Street, the northern boundary of the park. Leave the bus at Arguello Street and enter the park, keeping to the right. Continue to John F. Kennedy Drive, then turn left and you will quickly find yourself in front of a huge, ornate greenhouse, the Flower Conservatory.

The Conservatory is the oldest and most charming building in the park. It is a copy of the famous Kew Gardens near London and was originally designed for the private estate of James Lick near San Jose. Mr. Lick died before he could add this dazzling building to his collection. When the executors of his estate placed the materials for sale, a group of San Francisco citizens donated the purchase price and offered the materials to the park for erection.

Professional botanists may be disappointed because the Conservatory's collection of flowers and plants is not comparable to the great collections of the world. However, it does house a beautifully arranged and pleasing display.

Enhancing its tropical collection, which includes a pool

filled with water lilies of great size, is the Conservatory's fine assortment of hybrid orchids. Plus, the exhibition room in the west wing is changed almost monthly, featuring the outstanding blooms of the season. Many San Franciscans make it a point to visit this room with each change. We are told that all of the plants shown in the Conservatory are grown in the park's own nursery and none is obtained from the outside.

As you leave the Conservatory to return to Kennedy Drive, you will want to stroll among the outdoor flower beds, where you will also note a special display which usually spells out words of greeting to visiting organizations or proclaims civic fund-drives. The Conservatory is one of the city's showpieces which draws as many residents as out-of-town visitors.

To leave the area in front of the Flower Conservatory, cross Kennedy Drive by taking the underpass walkway, which places you on the south side of the thoroughfare. Turn right on exiting the tunnel and continue along the paved path marked "bike route." Soon you will find yourself in a small grove of giant ferns, enormous leafy plants with an otherworldly quality to them. Your walk also will take you past the entrance to the John McLaren Memorial Rhododendron Dell, marked by a small statue of the "creator" of Golden Gate Park. The dell itself is a 20-acre triangle, devoted almost exclusively to the park's most popular flower. If your visit to San Francisco just happens to be around late April, you must allow yourself a few minutes to investigate this incredible collection of hundreds of rainbow-hued varieties.

Continuing on past the entrance to the Rhododendron Dell, you soon reach (on your left) the entrance to a large complex of buildings, surrounding a music concourse with a band shell at the far end. This is the hub of the park's indoor activities. Circling the music concourse are:

The M. H. de Young Memorial Museum (directly to your right) which houses masterworks by El Greco, Rembrandt, Hals and Gainsborough, as well as America's Gilbert Stuart, John Singer Sargent and Thomas Eakins.

Eighteenth-century French paneled rooms, complete with their priceless furnishings, have been installed in one area; while in another, you can view the traditional arts of Africa, Oceania and the Americas. (Closed Monday and Tuesday.)

The Asian Art Museum: The Avery Brundage Collection is a two-story wing of the de Young, although it operates independently. The Brundage is one of the greatest collections of the art of oriental civilizations; I personally have only seen finer in Taiwan. For anyone interested in blue-and-white porcelains, jade and the other exquisite art forms developed centuries ago in the Orient, this museum is an absolute must! (Open daily.)

California Academy of Sciences (directly across the concourse from the de Young) houses an aquarium, hall of science, museum, and a planetarium. Most impressive, to me, is the Steinhart Aquarium with its 14,000-plus living aquatic habitants and its Fish Roundabout, the only aquarium of its kind in the Western Hemisphere. (Open daily.)

If today is blessed by San Francisco's typical benign sunshine and the idea of walking miles of museum corridors does not appeal to you as much as the sight and scent of newly cut grass and blossoming flowers, I will not blame you for by-passing these fine institutions for another visit on perhaps a more conducively foggy or rainy afternoon. However, we have allowed sufficient time in this area for at least a short visit, so you might use the time to rest your feet by sitting in front of a great master canvas.

If you want to look at more in the museums, don't try to "crack" all of them in a single day. The human eye cannot take in that much. So be selective—perhaps just sample the Brundage or visit my favorite El Greco. Today, we want to simply get the feel of this time and place in this park. You can always come back tomorrow or even on your next trip. After all, the object with sightseeing anywhere in the world is not to see how much you can see, but how well you can see it. And if your interests lie

in the tremendous wealth of art, history and all aspects
of nature and mankind which these buildings offer, you
might wish to make a mental note to schedule a return
visit sometime later in your stay.

4:00 p.m.   And now what would be more appropriate
after viewing the wonders of nature in the Rhododendron
Dell and the Flower Conservatory and the wonders of
creative man in a museum, than to see them brought
together in harmony in the magic of a Japanese tea
garden. Japanese garden designers, artisans of the highest
order, have a unique way of working with nature. In
densely populated Japan, where land is at a premium,
these geniuses are able to convert the smallest spaces into
miraculous retreats where one can contemplate nature.
Unfortunately, the serenity of a Japanese tea garden can
be upset by vast hordes of camera-toting visitors brought
in by polluting buses and this often happens at the
Japanese Tea Garden in Golden Gate Park. (Next to the
de Young Museum.)

   Yet, since it is late in the afternoon, hopefully the buses
have pushed on and you can wander at will through the
little pathways which wind in and around such delicately
refreshing beauties as golden carp swimming in still
ponds or tall bushes forever moving in a quiet breeze
which seems to be everywhere in this precious garden.

   And, if you are lucky enough to be in San Francisco
during the early spring (from the end of March through
April) the blossoming trees make the Tea Garden even
more magical. Well, no matter when you visit, you will
want to savor more of its Japanese flavor by making a
short stop at the little tea house, where you will be served
by authentically garbed Oriental waitresses. Only tea and
a few Japanese cookies are available. And be certain to
take all the leftover cookies with you; you will be needing
the crumbs in a few minutes.

4:30 p.m.   Leave the Japanese Tea Garden through the
main entrance and proceed to your right to the intersection. There turn right (the sign reads "To 19th Avenue"),

but in a few yards, take the first path off to the right. Keep on the path as it soon curves to the left around a huge tree. Ahead you will see a flight of concrete stairs. Climb them and on reaching the top keep to your right as you walk along Stow Lake.

Stow Lake is the largest lake in the park, and presents a scene of natural beauty and of people enjoying nature. Along its perimeter, you will see young and middle-aged joggers puffing along, elderly people in conversation with "park acquaintances" with whom they probably have shared the same bench every sunny afternoon for years, and children squealing with glee as they feed the geese, ducks and other water fowl who make Stow Lake their home. Be a child for a moment, yourself, and offer the birds the crumbs from those Japanese cookies.

In the center of Stow Lake, you will see a small island called Strawberry Hill, accessible by two bridges. It is one of my favorite places in the entire city. To reach this wonderful spot, simply follow the edge of the lake until you reach the large bridge. On crossing the bridge, turn to your left to the base of Huntington Falls.

Huntington Falls are totally man-made. And so is the hill from which they cascade some 75 feet. But no matter how "unnatural" this scene really is, it is still lovely. Especially if you don't look too closely at those big boulders which line the course of the falls. They too are man-made, because stones of this size do not exist in Golden Gate Park, which was entirely man-made itself. But more about that later. Right now, if you are up to it, why don't we climb the stairs alongside the falls which will take us to the top of the hill.

Along the way are breathing spots, which afford wonderful panoramas of the city. The higher you climb, the more beautiful the vista. At the very top, it's marvelous. Off to the right is the mass of buildings which make up the University of California Medical Center. Then directly ahead are the twin spires and dome of St. Ignatius Church, the focal point of the University of San Francisco. Further in the background is the dark monolith of the

Bank of America, my least favorite building in town! And seemingly next door is the Transamerica pyramid, the skyline's most distinctive skyscraper.

At the very top, no matter which way you turn another area of San Francisco presents itself. Also because it takes some effort to make the climb and because the hill itself seems to be a "secret place" for many locals, those who do come here appear to be extra friendly. Invariably you will be greeted by quiet hellos in recognition that you share their place.

If you do not think you want to make the effort to climb up, perhaps you can read about the park while you rest alongside the shore.

Unlike most city parks which were merely shaped out of existing woodlands, the entire area of Golden Gate Park used to be little more than sand dunes swept back from the Pacific Ocean beach, with no lakes and practically no vegetation. This great park, in all its apparent natural variety, was constructed out of 1000 acres of barren land. But do not think that everybody applauded the attempt. There were those who were skeptical and ridiculed the planners. They doubted the possibility of growing trees and grass on hills of sand which were constantly changing shape under driving ocean winds. But the miracle was accomplished!

Under the direction of William Hammond Hall, Park Superintendent in 1871, the first control of the sand was begun. Small boys were paid to go into the hills and collect seeds from wild plants which could grow in sand and provide anchorage.

In 1890, John McLaren became head of the park and remained so right up until his death in 1943. So great was his fame and his equally great contribution to the development of the park as we know it today, that many books on San Francisco have erred in crediting him as sole creator of this park raised out of sand. Though the original concept of Golden Gate Park was not Mr. McLaren's, its creative growth and brilliant nurturing were, for 53 years, in his hands. And it is because of him that Golden

Gate Park has no "Keep Off The Grass" signs. With the exception of newly seeded areas, every nook and cranny of the park is open to the public.

Because every bit of vegetation you see in Golden Gate Park had to be cultivated and brought in from elsewhere, the park today houses what is probably the largest variety of trees and plants from all over the world ever assembled in a city park. The only varieties missing are those which have defied all possible attempts at growth in this climate.

5:00 p.m. Now, it is time to head back to your hotel. If you have come by public transportation, all you need do is walk back to the cement stairs which had brought you up to the level of the lake. Descend them and turn to the left at the bottom. In a few minutes you will reach Kennedy Drive. Cross it and enter the Rose Garden. Walk directly through the Rose Garden and you will exit on the corner of Fulton and Park Presidio. Cross Park Presidio and board a Fulton #5 bus which will take you back downtown to Market Street. If you have driven to the park, simply retrace your steps back to your car, parked in front of the Flower Conservatory. Right behind the Conservatory, you can exit the park onto Arguello Boulevard; turn right onto Geary, and you are on your way to downtown San Francisco.

Note: You will notice that throughout this book, you are given drive-yourself and bus transportation directions. However, you can certainly substitute taxis. San Francisco has many taxi cab companies, all charging the same rate. For the best service, my personal preferences are the De Soto Cab Company (673-1414) and Luxor Cabs (552-4040). Be forewarned, though, that cab fares in San Francisco are probably among the highest in the nation. Of course, if you have ridden taxis in New York City, you may be glad to pay the extra charge in return for the warm courtesy for which San Francisco cab drivers are well known. They still tell the story of the New Yorker who fainted when a

San Francisco cab driver thanked him for a tip, only to be revived and then faint again when the same cab driver opened the door and helped him out with his packages!

In fact, this might be a good place to stop and talk about courtesy, because it is one of the first things visitors notice about San Francisco. Naturally, San Franciscans are human, too, and there are exceptions. But, by and large, San Franciscans are among the most polite people in the United States, and certainly the friendliest. This means that even if you are visiting here alone, you probably will enjoy your stay more than you would in most other cities. Do not be surprised if the very proper-looking lady sitting next to you on the cable car starts a conversation. And, of course, do not hesitate to start one yourself.

If you find yourself standing on the outside of one of our cable cars with an armload of packages, the lady or gentleman seated in front of you most likely will insist on holding the packages for you. This is common custom here and you should not refuse the invitation although, like most visitors, you may find it a bit startling at first!

6:30 p.m. Most American cities, especially tourist-conscious ones, have some kind of historic edifice which has been converted into a shopping-dining complex. San Francisco has two exceptional examples within a few blocks of one another—The Cannery and Ghirardelli Square. The latter, which happens to be my favorite, was designed as a factory complex in 1893; and for 70 years, this 2½-acre site was the home of the Ghirardelli Chocolate Company. When the chocolate makers moved, the massive brick complex could have been leveled to make way for another high rise for the well-heeled. But thanks to civic-minded William Matson Roth, the ancient buildings marked by the quaint clock tower, curiously a copy of the Chateau Blois in France, were converted into a warren of shops and eateries, opening onto a sunny piazza with another whimsical Ruth Asawa fountain. As

I understand it, the original shops and restaurants came to the square by invitation only. Shops range from quality imported gourmet items, exotic kites, hand-crafted jewelry to the finest in Scandinavian household items, all in good taste.

And good taste is also a product of several of the square's many restaurants. Last night I suggested the excellent Paprikas Fono, and for this evening I present two more of its best for your selection. Although they differ widely in their styles of cuisine, both do offer Bay views from at least some of their tables.

8:00 p.m.   The Mandarin, Ghirardelli Square (673-8812; open every day for lunch and dinner; reservations advised), is probably the most beautiful Chinese restaurant in San Francisco. And to knowledgeable restaurant-goers, it is much more than that. Before Mme. Chiang opened her original Mandarin in a small cubbyhole far removed aesthetically and physically from this sumptuous site, San Francisco knew little of Chinese cooking other than Cantonese. In fact, just about 99% of all Chinese restaurants in America were Cantonese. Today, the Bay Area hosts hordes of restaurants devoted to the cuisines of Peking, Szechwan, Hunan and Shanghai; and invariably, you will find in their kitchens a Mandarin "graduate." Yet, to me, The Mandarin still retains its unrivaled preeminence.

And the best way to enjoy its pan-China cuisine is to ask to speak to either Mme. Chiang or her knowledgeable manager, Mr. Lin Chien, when you call for your reservations. Indicate that you are seriously interested in the finest in Chinese cuisine and wish assistance in planning your dinner. The Mandarin can be an exciting restaurant experience and it is well worth this extra effort.

To help you order, here are some favorites: Chiao-tzu, meat-filled steamed dumplings crisply fried on one side; Stuffed Cucumber Soup; Minced Squab in Lettuce Cups, a marvelous marriage of flavors and textures; Smoked Tea Duck; and for dessert, Glazed Bananas with a hot syrup coating which crystallizes when the bananas are dunked into ice water. If you are not familiar with fiery Szechwan cuisine order a dish such as Green Beans in Szechwan sauce. It can make Tex-Mex chili seem cool in comparison. When at peak performance (alas, there can be lapses) the Mandarin is one of San Francisco's great restaurants—with prices to match.

Modesto Lanzone's, Ghirardelli Square (771-2880; open for dinner nightly except Monday; lunch served Tuesday through Friday; reservations a must). Modesto Lanzone is without doubt the most successful Italian restaurateur in San Francisco. His two locations—the other in Opera Plaza—enjoy almost always turn-away business. What you will find is generally excellent Italian cooking, especially in the pasta department, with some variability creeping into the main courses.

To start, do not miss the Insalate di Mare, a memorable mixture of bay shrimp and ringlets of squid in an understated but nicely piquant vinaigrette. Split an order for two. If there are three or four in your party, also order a portion of Cold Stuffed Breast of Veal. Your pasta course may likewise be split for two, but since this is where Modesto excels, I find it hard to share my favorite, the deceptively simple Linguine with Marinara Sauce. Most Italian restaurants in America mercilessly overcook their tomato sauce to an acid bath. But Modesto's is gloriously fresh, while the pasta is correctly "al dente." The Agnolotti, small crescents of stuffed pasta in a cream sauce, are top notch. And for something more exotic, try the Panzotti, spinach-ricotta cheese pillows in an elegant cream sauce crunchy with minced walnuts.

One of my favorite dishes here is the classic Chicken Cacciatore. Seemingly made to order, it outranks most local versions and demonstrates what a revelation in flavors this much maligned dish can be, when properly done. Veal dishes like the Picatta are acceptably handled, but not stunningly. Vegetables are invariably fresh. If you still can manage a rich dessert, try that sinfully caloric Genovese cake, Sacripantina, followed by a velvety espresso. And for an after-dinner drink, you might try the

Italian equivalent of white lightning, grappa. Fairly expensive.

NOTE: If during your stay you attend any evening performances at either the Opera House or Davies Symphony Hall, you might wish to try Modesto Lanzone's in Opera Plaza, 601 Van Ness Avenue (928-0400; dinners nightly except Sunday; reservations advised). While some dishes are found on both menus, the Opera Plaza kitchen tends toward some more adventuresome pastas, in which it also shines. For example, the Gnocchi Verdi are feathery little spinachy pasta puffs drenched in melted butter. And evening specials, such as a sublime Cappeletti with Clams make me often opt for pasta as a main course, thereby avoiding potential main-course pitfalls, such as a Vitello Dore, which was more like veal fu yung! The restaurant is almost equally noted for its vast collection of modern art. Although frankly I find the Arneson bust of Modesto in the entranceway repulsive. But I close my eyes in order to indulge in those superb pastas!

Chez Michel, 804 North Point at Hyde Street (771-6077; dinner served nightly except Monday; reservations advised) is a wonderful chic bistro just one block from Ghirardelli Square. To me it's a place where I know I will enjoy fine French cuisine, but in a relaxed cozy atmosphere. The ceiling is an enormous tentlike, illuminated psychedelic quilt; there are no tablecloths just place mats; candlelight and flowers further mellow the mood.

The printed menu is not vast, nevertheless it presents an enticing variety, balancing the classic with the *au courant*. However, at times I ignore it completely, if the *menu degustation* catches my fancy. Years ago, most restaurants, expecially those in San Francisco, served "complete dinners"—big, set multi-course affairs. But as times changed and costs rose, the complete dinner fell into disrepute; many of the courses deteriorated into blatant fillers—limp salads, cheerless soups.

But with the advent of *nouvelle cuisine*, the *menu*

degustation came into vogue. While it is indeed a "complete dinner", it is actually one composed of smaller portions, almost samplings, which are meant to showcase the chef's creativity, not gorge the dinner. Chez Michel presents such a *menu degustation*, which often combines smaller portions of regular menu offerings with nightly specials.

For example, one evening dinner began beautifully with a Tartare of Tuna in which the ground raw tuna was lightly moistenend with olive oil and touched with lemon. Served with freshly toasted bread, it was an intriguing precursor to a glowing Red Snapper Filet, sauvely sauteed, covered with pre-cooked (to reduce their violence) garlic slivers and decorated with quasi-raw brilliant green pea pods. After two elusively fragile dishes such as these, the Confit of Duck was just perfect. This twice-cooked duck dish presents a robust flavor, which is ideally congenial with that of the potato pancake wedge on which it rests and the accompanying slaw of red cabbage. A not too adventuresome and incorrectly chilled cheese course followed. For a finale: a cumulous fresh pear mousse was a delectable isle in a dark chocolate-sauce sea. Intriguing cuisine in a charming *intime* restaurant. I guess you would say expensive, but not in the luxury price bracket.

10:00 p.m.   After a full day of window shopping and park strolling, I would not imagine you would desire anything other than a comfortable bed right now. However, if you still feel like "going," the Buena Vista is only a block away from any one of these three restaurants. And you might want to drop in before boarding your cable car to take you back downtown. Have an Irish Coffee for me!

Your Third Perfect Day Schedule

9:00 a.m. While you are having your morning coffee, why don't you write some of those postcards?

10:00 a.m. Drive or take a bus to the Golden Gate Bridge for a short stroll on the world-famous span. It may no longer be the world's longest single span, but it certainly is the most beautiful!

10:45 a.m. Continue on, either by car or bus, to picturesque Sausalito with its dramatic view of San Francisco.

12:30 p.m. After a walk through Sausalito, lunch right on the water with a full view of the Bay or in the parlor of a former house of ill repute—no, not Sally Stanford's!

2:00 p.m. Off to marvelous Muir Woods, natural habitat of our famed giant redwoods.

4:00 p.m. Drive back across the Golden Gate. If you took a bus over, you can now enjoy an early cocktail on the ferry as it carries you back across the Bay to San Francisco.

6:00 p.m. Rest at your hotel or finish off those postcards.

8:00 p.m. Choose between Morocco's cumin-accented cuisine or the tantalizing flavors of Thailand. In either case, wear comfortable clothes, because you will be sitting almost on the floor!

10:00 p.m. For laughs try one of our many comedy clubs. Who knows?—Robin Williams might be on.

The Third Day of Your

One Perfect Week in San Francisco

9:00 a.m. If today is not a Monday, our plans are to leave town. This delightful little trip will enable you to see at very close hand the Golden Gate Bridge (in fact, you will cross it), the unique hillside town of Sausalito with its intriguing shops (many of which close on Mondays) and sweeping panorama of San Francisco, plus the giant redwood trees of Muir Woods. It is a trip you can make by car or a combination of bus, taxi and ferry boat. So have just a light breakfast at your hotel. And it's as good a time as any to write a couple of those promised post cards.

10:00 a.m. Breakfast over, let's begin our trip. First, let me give directions for those wishing to drive. Find Franklin Street (it runs parallel to Van Ness). On Franklin (here I assume you are staying in the downtown area) turn right. Actually, you have to, since Franklin is one way! As you proceed down Franklin, you will pass a few choice examples of Victorian homes, such as the Haas-Lilienthal House at number 2007 on your left. Built in 1886 in the Queen Anne style, it survived the '06 fire and is now open as a museum (call 441-3004 for tour information, if you are interested in seeing its interior). Another beautiful example in the Italianate style is on the far right corner of Franklin and Pacific. When you reach Lombard Street, turn left and proceed to the bridge, turning right into the "View Area" immediately prior to the toll plaza.

The Golden Gate Bridge was, for many years, known as the longest single-span suspension bridge in the world—4,200 feet between its towers. However, its length is not the chief reason for its fame. Other cities may build larger bridges or taller ones, but I doubt if they will ever build a more beautiful one. For to do so, they would have to match the setting—the beautiful coastlines on both sides, the majestic hills of Marin on the north, the city of San Francisco sparkling like a jewel on the south. They would have to build a machine to create great billowy banks of fog for stunning visual effects. They would have to make certain their calculations produce a graceful, simple and noble shape. And then they would have to paint their bridge red, a daring move which is usually a great surprise to visitors who see it for the first time.

And so, if the Golden Gate Bridge has lost its title as the longest single-span suspension bridge in the world, it has not lost first place for grandeur and beauty.

Incidentally, if you simply must have statistics, here they are: The Golden Gate Bridge was first opened to pedestrian traffic on May 27, 1937, when 202,000 people thronged across it. The next day, vehicular traffic began. The bridge is 8,940 feet long and its pillars tower 746 feet above high tide. At the center, you find yourself 220 feet above low water which explains its attraction to suicides. The tops of the towers rise above the water approximately the same height as a 65-story building. But there are no statistics for the hours of pleasure it has provided both visitors who gasp at its breathtaking beauty upon first seeing it, and residents who cross it twice a day but never seem to tire of its beauty.

If there are children in your party, you now have an excellent chance to enjoy one of the delights of San Francisco while at the same time help your youngsters blow off steam—you can walk across the Golden Gate Bridge to the view area on the Marin County side. (Note: If your party is split between the younger and older generations, part of your group may wish to drive the car across, meeting the walking contingent at the lookout point on the other side. However, please be warned that it is a long walk and you are not advised to attempt it unless you are dressed warmly and have a good deal of stamina.)

10:45 a.m. After taking your fill of the sweep and

majesty of this awe-inspiring structure and the fresh ocean breeze in your lungs, it is time to proceed to our next destination—Sausalito. Simply drive across the span and take the Alexander Avenue exit to the right. The long downward drive from the highway into Sausalito is a beautiful one. On one side are the grass-covered, rolling hills of Marin, seemingly far removed from urban life; while on the other, you can catch glimpses of the towers of downtown San Francisco. A "Slow to 15" sign alerts you to the fact you are entering Sausalito. And slowing down here is a good idea for it will also enable you to view the variety of houses perched on the hills above you. Up there, real estate prices are as spectacular as their picture-window views. Find a parking space near Second and Main Streets, if you are lucky. If you cannot find one, proceed ahead to the town square, where you will find a public parking area nearby. And now let me escort those coming over by bus.

If you are making the trip by bus, find Van Ness Avenue. On Van Ness you will find several stops of the Golden Gate Transit line (call 332-6600 for schedule information). Their stops are marked by green, red and blue signs. You will find them on the corners of Van Ness and Geary, Sutter, Clay and Union. (Note: The Golden Gate Transit buses are not part of the San Francisco Municipal bus system, so you should be looking for the ones which are predominantly white and green, bearing the same tri-color insignia as the bus stop sign.) On boarding the bus, ask the driver to let you off at the Golden Gate Bridge toll plaza so you can view the bridge as did those going by car.

If you wish to walk across the span, you can do so and pick up a bus to Sausalito on the other side. However, because of the location of the bus stop on the Marin County side, you will be walking a good two miles. If you do not wish to make this trek, after walking a ways out on the bridge, simply return to the spot where you got off and catch the next bus for Sausalito, asking the driver for the Second and Main Street stop.

Whether you came by car or bus, you are now at Second and Main. You will want to walk from here down Main Street to the boardwalk under which the waters of the Bay gently lap. The restaurant here on the corner of Main and the boardwalk was once the famed Valhalla restaurant, operated until her death by Sally Stanford, one of Sausalito's great characters. Thousands of words have been written about Sally Stanford and her unique checkered career. Years ago—World War II days—the name Sally Stanford was synonymous with San Francisco's shady nightlife; she was the proud madam of the town's most elegant bordello. Later, Sally went "legit," and opened the Valhalla in Sausalito. Probably as a tongue-in-cheek reminder of her past, a red light always burned in an upstairs window. Then, in 1975, Sally Stanford achieved what she had been trying to do for many years— she became mayor of Sausalito. I like to think that Sally and her career could only have happened in places like San Francisco and Sausalito.

A walk along the boardwalk will lead right onto Bridgeway, the main street of Sausalito. Strolling along Bridgeway towards the business district is a lovely walk. That rock on your right in the water which resembles a sea lion is not, of course, a natural phenomenon shaped by the sea into a likeness of the animal—but rather a stone carving. And one of the town's most amusing posters is a photo of an actual seal posing jubilantly atop his stone likeness. At just about this point, a glance up the hill on your left will reveal a house looking somewhat like the truncated foundation for a fortress. Had not the indignation of some townspeople been brought to bear upon William Randolph Hearst, Sr., the building might have been completed and Sausalito could very well have been the possessor of a famed castle similar to San Simeon. But Mr. Hearst was invited to leave town by a delegation of husbands and fathers at the insistence of their wives who disapproved of Mr. Hearst's moral standards.

Those of you who came over by bus will have to decide

on which side of Bridgeway to walk. On the left are dozens of little shops, cluttered with the latest fashion, handcrafted jewelry and the most unusual in antiques. On the right are intrepid fishermen hoping to pull something from the lapping Bay waters. Those of you who drove over will have to return to your car by the same route, so you will be able to cover both sides of the street.

Soon you will come upon the town square with its two unusual and somewhat incongruous elephant statues to greet you. These elephants and that nearby fountain were originally part of the Panama-Pacific International Exposition held in San Francisco in 1915, and were donated to the city of Sausalito after the close of the Exposition.

Almost across the street is the Village Fair, a "must-see" for any visitor. The structure was an abandoned garage until it was converted into a showcase for several independent little shops. It is sort of a mini-Ghirardelli Square, although many years older. The Village Fair shopping complex was a natural for Sausalito, since the town was long famous for its local craftsmen and artisans. It is a totally delightful maze and don't hurry through—there are many things to see and buy.

12:30 p.m.   Choosing a luncheon spot in Sausalito for this edition of the guide was a lot easier task than for previous editions thanks to the appearance of a daring young chef in the newly expanded Casa Madrona Hotel. However, lunch here can be a little costly, and although the dining room does have a beautiful view it does not include the majestic San Francisco skyline. Therefore, what I will offer you is your choice of three lunch spots from which you may chose.

The Casa Madrona, 801 Bridgeway, (331-5888; open for lunch Monday through Friday; for dinner Monday through Saturday; reservations advised) is far and away my first choice.

After you enter the Casa Madrona Hotel on Bridgeway, you take an elevator to an upper floor, walk up two flights of stairs through a charming flower garden and enter what was once an old bordello. The comfortable cheery dining room retains some of the Victorian charm of its past. But the main focus is on the lovely view of Belvedere and Angel Island, but not San Francisco, to be seen through huge windows. There is also an outdoor terrace, which at the moment cannot be used for lunch, due to some city ordinance. Why? Don't ask me!

But this room is an especially nostalgic one for me. For it was here that our careers as restaurant critics were launched and a previously unknown area of consumer-oriented journalism created. You see, back in 1967, restaurant criticism *per se* did not exist. For years, there had been restaurant ratings, as those published by France's Michelin Tire Company to encourage people to use their product by driving out to restaurants in the country. And of course there were puff-piece articles on dining out, penned by restaurant *writers*, such as gourmand Lucius Beebe. But seldom did a harsh word about a restaurant ever see printer's ink.

Therefore, when we decided to create a monthly restaurant guide, in which we would present our unbiased findings after anonymously visiting restaurants, we were—like Abner Doubleday—inventing a game that had never previously been played. Thus, not only did our *Private Guide to Restaurants* become America's first and most successful publication devoted to restaurant reviews, but it also spawned a type of journalism that is now practiced in magazines and newspapers throughout the country.

Anyhow, in the ensuing twenty years, this room has changed quite a bit and happily the cuisine even more so. Today, the Casa Madrona presents the nouvelle-California creations of one of our "young Turk" chefs. Even though he can commit some almost inexplicable errors, his batting average is quite high. And he can belt some out-of-the-park homers!

For example, his Manila Clams Steamed with Ginger, Leek and Carrots are sublime! These clams, supposedly from the Oregon Coast, were new to me and rival most Eastern ones. Some of the ginger-scented steaming liquid has been lightly thickened with cream and filled with semi-raw threads of leek and carrot. His Potato Pancake with Golden Caviar and Creme Fraiche is another solid hit. Upon one large potato pancake, its edge slightly browned and lacy in a Florentine cookie fashion, is a spread of thick fresh cream and a truly generous helping of excellent golden caviar. The subtlety of the pancake and cream allows you to fully savor the caviar's delicate flavor. Beautiful!

For a main course, the Swordfish with Beurre Blanc and Beurre Rouge, presents a peerlessly cooked fish, moated by the pale white-butter sauce, traced with patterns of the wine-enriched red-butter sauce. Perfect carrots, a just-done new potato and the youngest of string beans are the garnishes. However, a Grilled Chicken Breast with Fresh Herbs is bungled. The almost charred skin is appealingly parchment crisp, but beneath the meat is almost raw. It's returned to the kitchen for correction. But you could not fault the tender spinach leaves, so under-done they cleanse your teeth.

The kitchen makes a quick comeback with a delicious sable-dough fresh fruit tart and a cake constructed of layers of hazel-nut meringue and hazel-nut buttercream.

Even with errors like the chicken, I regard Casa Madrona as the most interesting and finest restaurant in Sausalito. And when you serve this intriguing style of cuisine in front of that view, what more could one ask? Expensive.

Horizons, 558 Bridgeway (331-3232; open daily for lunch and dinner), claims our attention primarily for its beautiful situation, just a few feet above the lapping waters of San Francisco Bay. From its outdoor deck, you can watch the seagulls perform with the sweeping skyline of San Francisco as their backdrop. However, should the weather be too chilly, with dense fog not only grounding the·birds but blotting out the spectacular view, you can lunch indoors in the midst of a forest of hanging ferns and highly polished wood. The food will be serviceable. The somewhat spicier-than-most Guacamole is pleasant, not the oft-encountered overmashed mush but texture with avocado chunks. But the tortilla chips are mundanely commerical.

Best bet for a main course is usually a fresh fish in season, such as Petrale Sole or Salmon. Well handled fresh vegetables are nicely done. The hamburger is of healthy size and is preceded by a pleasant small salad. More complicated cooking can prove to be somewhat chancy. A Mud Pie, made with Haagen-Dazs' superb coffee ice cream, is about the extent of the kitchen's creativity in that department. Moderate prices.

The Alta Mira Hotel, 125 Bulkley (332-1350; open daily for breakfast, lunch and dinner) because of its prime hillside site offers an even more spectacular panorama of San Francisco and just about the entire Bay. On a warm day, the vast open deck, festive with colorful umbrellas, gives the place the air of a splendid hotel on the Italian Riviera. Would that the food completed the picture! But alas over the years the Alta Mira's culinary offerings have steadily declined. Even their Coquette Salad, which I once could commend, is now barely passable. The last time I sampled one it consisted of enough lettuce to feed a rabbit hutch, some mediocre sliced turkey, and a sparse fruit garnish. As for their cooked dishes, I can no longer tolerate them. To reach the Alta Mira, climb the staircase marked Excelsior Lane, located next to the Wells Fargo Bank opposite the town square. The entrance to the hotel is at the end of the shaded lane.

So the decision on where to lunch is entirely yours. Let your taste in food, your pocketbook and the weather be your guides.

2:00 p.m.   It is now time to finish off the final delectable crumb of that Casa Madrona dessert or quit basking in the sun on the deck of either Horizons or the Alta Mira, and head on to the Muir Woods National Monument. Again, allow me to give directions to those going by car. Retrace your steps back along Bridgeway to your car; then drive through the town, heading north. The mountain top you see ahead of you is Mount Tamalpais (2604 feet). Muir Woods is located at the bottom of its southern slope.

As you are exiting Sausalito, follow the sign indicating "Highway 101—Eureka". Stay in the right lane and take the first turnoff which is marked "Mill Valley, Stinson Beach, Route 1." Route 1 soon begins to cut through eucalyptus groves and curves over the rolling hillside. You will leave Route 1 at a turn-off marked "Muir Woods 3 miles."

If you do not have a car, there are other means by which you can reach Muir Woods. The Gray Line (771-4000) runs daily bus tours from San Francisco to the woods, passing through Sausalito on the return trip. And there are many other tour services, many using those little mini-buses, which will also take you to Muir Woods with some shopping-browsing time in Sausalito included in their packages. However, if you want to be more foot-loose and dictate your own time schedule, you can easily take a taxi to the woods from Sausalito. It's not all that expensive, especially if there are four or five in your party. The Sausalito Yellow Cab Company (332-2200) does run a special taxi service to the woods. The fare is about $40 for up to five persons, and includes the round-trip cab ride, along with approximately 40 minutes at the park. But whether you go by tour bus, by automobile or by taxi, you simply must go to Muir Woods.

Named in honor of the famed naturalist-conservationist-writer, John Muir, Muir Woods is the closest refuge to San Francisco of the giant sequoia, the redwood—the world's tallest living thing. Every great city has its so-called tourist attractions. These are usually termed "must-see's." In fact, I myself used that term a few pages back. However, Muir Woods is not just a "must-see," it is a "must-experience!" I don't imagine many San Francisco residents spend a morning or afternoon going through Muir Woods on their own. Yet, it is amazing how eagerly they will volunteer to show visitors this beautiful park. Like residents of all cities, I guess we feel somewhat self-conscious about frequenting sightseeing spots. But just provide the excuse and I, for one, would be glad to spend many quiet hours in Muir Woods.

Naturally, the main attraction is the redwood tree, that unbelievably tall and majestic creation of nature. Although not the largest in the West, the ones which you are looking at rise an impressive 250 feet or more and reach a diameter of 17 feet. To see these trees would be reward enough, particularly at a point so close to the city of San Francisco. But Muir Woods offers more than this. It offers a natural habitat for the redwood—an exquisite environment of surrounding companion shrubs which have remained faithful to these great trees for centuries.

Take time to walk back into the woods a ways. You will be surprised how quickly you can detach yourself from the hub-bub of an arriving busload, most of whom head straight for the gift shop. Walk back along the trail and find yourself a rippling brook and listen to its mellow sound for a while. Here, to me, the towering trees impart a cathedral aura, and the silence evokes a religious appreciation for life. If you want to ponder the insignificance of man, just sit quietly and consider the fact that some of these trees were already alive before Christ.

Also, while we are in the park, I think it appropriate to mention how thankful we should be to our National Park Service. Just notice the way in which they have carefully, but unobtrusively, marked out the paths and sights of interest, and have included a special Miwok Braille Trail for the blind.

If you are interested in hiking, this area of Marin County offers a wealth of well-marked trails. Along them in the spring you will discover a wild-flower wonderland—Douglas iris, trillium, monkey flowers, blue-eyed grass, Indian paint brush, lupine, and literally dozens of others, including, of course, the California poppy. And often as you hike along a Mount Tamalpais trail, you will look up from examining a crimson Indian warrior, to gaze at the dramatic skyline of San Francisco far off in the distance. So if you are a hiker or even just a good walker, you should plan to experience the trails of Mount Tamalpais some time during your stay. Trail maps and guides are available right here in the gift shop at Muir Woods.

4:00 p.m. If you came by car, you can experience the park as long as you wish, at least until sunset which is the closing hour. However, for those of you who came either by cab or bus, it is now time to leave. By automobile, simply exit from the park following the well-marked signs back to San Francisco. Your taxi will take you back to Sausalito's town square. Here, you should check the ferry schedule posted at the ferry dock on the Bay side of the town square (or telephone 332-6600) for the next departure to San Francisco.

If during the day, you have envied those who were able to travel by car, you should feel much better making your way back by ferry. For while they are driving the 17 freeway miles back to San Francisco, you can relax on the upper deck of the ship, a drink in one hand (cocktails are *de rigueur* on the Bay for many ferry commuters), tossing potato chip crumbs to the hovering gulls with the other. And the Bay at this time of day can be fantastic! For those of you who cannot make the ferry trip today, I have scheduled a Bay cruise for later in your week. No matter how you manage it, a trip on San Francisco Bay should not be missed.

On docking at the San Francisco side, at the old, historic Ferry Building, you might wish to walk across the Embarcadero and drop into the Hyatt Regency Hotel. If you have never seen one of these incredible multi-storied Hyatt lobbies, this is an awesome example—complete with fountains, huge sculptures, and elevators of Buck Rogers design. You might wish another cocktail in the revolving Equinox Room (open from 11 a.m. to 1:30 a.m.) at the top. Then, it is either a cab or public transportation back to your hotel.

6:00 p.m. I am certain a couple hours of rest after your long day would be welcome right now. Back in your hotel, you can catch the evening TV news and find out what the world has been doing, or write those post-cards—it's now or never!

8:00 p.m. Tonight's two dinner selections are very casual, very moderately priced and very exotic. In both restaurants you sit nearly on the floor, and in one you will eat with your bare hands. All set?

Khan Toke, 5937 Geary Blvd. near 24th Ave. (668-6654; open daily for dinner only; reservations advised), gives you a quick trip to fabled Thailand to experience not only its lovely cuisine but also its gracious manner of dining. Here you remove your shoes on entering and are seated on cushions at low lacquered tables, where you can relish the delicate, at times winsome, at times fiery cuisine. Start with the Look Chin Moo Yang. That's pork balls to the rest of us. Into rice paper discs, you place a piece of pork ball, peanuts, hot pepper, ginger, garlic and a dribbling of tamarind sauce. Then pop the whole thing into your mouth, sit back and enjoy a veritable kaleidoscope of flavors and textures. Another popular Thai appetizer is Tod Mun, fish cakes covered in a piquant cucumber sauce.

For main courses (order Chinese style) do not miss the Kay Yang, marinated barbecued chicken with a honey of a honey sauce, and the Imperial Duck, succulent meat under a cracklingly crisp, deep-fried coat. To sample Thai curry, the Mus-A-Mun is a must: beef in a coconut milk-red curry capable of converting even die-hard curry haters. The Fried Banana for dessert is as good as this dish can get. Thai beer provides the perfect foil to dampen some of the spiciness you will encounter on this fascinating visit to Bangkok by the Bay. (To reach Khan Toke, simply drive out Geary St.—or take a #38 bus—right to its door.)

El Mansour, 3123 Clement St. at 32nd Ave. (751-2312; open daily for dinner only; reservations advised) is a fine, and surprisingly modestly priced, exponent of another of the world's more exotic cuisines, that of Morocco. Since Moroccan dining is more than just a pleasure for the ᵔalate but rather a multi-sensory experience, I strongly recommend you take along two necessities. The first is a completely open mind, one that will not hamper your enjoyment of eating the food with your bare hands; in keeping with the true Moroccan dining experience, forks and knives are not presented. Your open mind also will help open your palate to such flavor marriages as cinnamon and sugar used to season chicken, in addition to the heady accents of cumin. The second requisite is comfortable, casual dress (ties are out!) as you will be sitting on low, soft ottomans or lolling back on cushions.

Once at El Mansour, all you need do is choose your main dish because all other courses are set along standard Moroccan lines. You start with Harira, a spicy lentil-lamb soup which you drink directly from the bowl. Next comes an array of Moroccan salads—cucumber, tomato, carrot and cumin-laced eggplant. They are eaten with chunks of bread employed shovel-fashion. Then you are served the great *piece de resistance*—Bastela, a hot, paper-thin filo-dough pie encasing a mad mixture of chicken, eggs and nuts all scented with cinnamon and spices and sweetened with sugar. The taste is so addictive, you will find yourself risking singed fingers to eat it quickly. For a main course, I favor the unusually succulent Chicken with Lemon. Other people in your party may opt for any of the many lamb dishes, Lamb and Almonds being my preference; or for the excellent Couscous, a steaming plate of semolina topped with an assortment of vegetables and lamb. But to me, Moroccan dining is a communal experience so why not have everyone order a different main course and all share in, no holds barred! It may be messy, but it's great fun. Your fingers will become even stickier as you sample your dessert of a deep-fried, honey-glazed banana. This seems to me more Indonesian than Moroccan, but it is delicious. Sweet green mint tea—the finale to any meal or business deal in Morocco—completes your feast. (To reach El Mansour by car, simply drive out Geary to 32nd Avenue and turn right one block to Clement. Or to go by bus from the Union Square area, simply board a Clement #2 bus on Sutter St.—one block north of Union Square—and it will deliver you almost to the door of El Mansour.)

10:00 p.m.   A very popular form of entertainment in San Francisco is its comedy clubs. Here fledgling comedians try out their routines, hopeful that someday they can perform the polished version for Johnny Carson's viewers. And often, comedy greats like Robin Williams have been know to drop by unexpectedly to test some of their new acts. Again, the best place to get a current reading on who is appearing where around town and in the entire Bay Area is in the Date Book Section of the Sunday San Francisco *Examiner & Chronicle.* There you will find listings of all jazz joints, nightclubs, and music events as well.

Your Fourth Perfect Day Schedule

9:30 a.m. A Spartan juice-and-coffee breakfast is what's recommended this morning before we embark on our tour through . . .

10:00 a.m. Chinatown! The largest in the Western world. I will take you on a personally conducted mini-tour, pointing out where to buy wicker or woks. Or the finest won ton if you wish to lunch at a back-street noodle shop. Or sample a wonderful style of Chinese cuisine you probably never have heard of—Hakka.

2:00 p.m. Rest your feet while you give your eyes and ears a treat at either a performance of the symphony, opera, theater or even a good movie. Yes, I recommend a movie as an ideal sightseeing breather!

5:00 p.m. Wile away the cocktail hour in a downtown aerie from which you can watch the commuter traffic struggle home.

7:30 p.m. Dine at the city's finest California-style grill; indulge in fanciful French nouvelle cuisine; just dig into a superb slab of prime rib of beef. Those are your choices in my three restaurant recommendations for tonight.

10:00 p.m. Sprawl in front of your hotel TV to see if you can catch one of the San Francisco based shows—by now, you should know your way around better than the movie cameras! Tomorrow brings Japantown and Union Street.

The Fourth Day of Your

One Perfect Week in San Francisco

9:30 a.m. If you followed my night-club going recommendation last night, you should appreciate this slightly delayed opening of your Fourth Perfect Day. Try to forgo breakfast or at least limit it to a Spartan juice-and-coffee because we have a very exciting Chinese lunch planned at noon.

10:00 a.m. Because I will personally conduct you through San Francisco's world-famous Chinatown, it is best we begin at that quarter's official entrance—the ornate Chinese gate on the corner of Bush and Grant. If you are staying either on Nob Hill or in the Union Square area, it is only a short walk or cab ride. In fact, the reason our Chinatown is so popular for shopping and dining with localites as well as visitors is that it is centrally located, immediately adjacent to the downtown hub of the city. This, for example, is not the case in New York where you must undertake a lengthy subway or cab ride far from midtown Manhattan. So now it's off to Chinatown. Oh, yes, bring along those postcards you wrote yesterday. We will pass a post office where you can buy stamps at their face values, and thus avoid being ripped off by those exorbitantly priced postage machines.

As we pass through the Chinatown gate, try not to notice those two hamburger eateries blighting the entrance on both sides. Instead, you might wish to hum the melody from "Flower Drum Song"—"Grant Avenue, San Francisco, U.S.A"—for that is indeed the street on which we will be concentrating this morning. Let us start up the right-hand side.

With every new edition of this guide, I find that I must delete yet another ancient shop or two along our Grant

Avenue route. The reason is simple: Chinatown is prime real estate and often, after the sale of a building, long-time shop owners find their rents increased by astronomical leaps. Thus, the former quaint little bead shop or antique shop is now a bank or McDonald's. Nevertheless, there is still a wonderful excitement and color to Chinatown that should not be missed.

Our first stop will be at Tai Chong, 506 Grant. This place has everything, so look carefully. Amidst the "tourist trinkets," you will often find some very attractive items such as superior carved wooden corners for doorways, and small art objects. And among the gaudy satins, you might even discover some old silks which, today, are nearly unobtainable.

Gumling Importing Company, 544 Grant, is an attractive little shop with a commendable jewelry selection. (If you are considering serious jade purchases, I will also have some other recommendations later on.) Take a look at the ladies' oriental kimonos and small art objects.

Old St. Mary's Church, on the corner of Grant and California, dates from 1854. The original shell of brick, most of which was quarried in China and shipped in sailing vessels across the vast Pacific, withstood the quake which triggered the '06 fire, but the interior was totally gutted. Today, this charming church holds a special place in the affections of all San Franciscans. Opposite the church on California Street is St. Mary's Square, a pleasant sunning spot for financial-district lunchers, watched over by Benny Bufano's imposing statue of Sun Yat Sen.

The Canton Bazaar, 616 Grant, is a large Chinese emporium where the unpracticed eye can have difficulty separating the antiques from the mass-made, although the price tags might be considered clues. If you are making a serious purchase, you may wish to buy subject to an impartial appraisal, a worthwhile caution in any shop.

Lun On, 771 Sacramento just below Grant, is an old established specialist in bamboo and rattan. An ideal take-home purchase is a bamboo food protector for outdoor entertaining. Further down Sacramento Street at

755, you will find an unusual building housing the Nam Kue Elementary School. Now, back up to Grant Avenue and continue for one block to Clay Street.

Here we will have a short climb up Clay Street for one block to Stockton Street. On that corner you will see a U.S. Post Office from which you can mail those post-cards. But more important, immediately next door, at 855 Stockton Street, you will uncover the entrance to the Taoist Kong Chow Temple (take the elevator at the rear of the lobby to the fourth floor). This is an active temple where you will find worshipers burning incense and sweet oils as offerings to Kwan Ti. For a dollar, you can have your fortune told—it is invariably a rosy one. The temple with its ornately carved altar is fascinating, and so is the cityscape from its terrace. After enjoying the temple, return back down Clay Street for a half block to Waverly Place and turn left.

This block of Waverly is lined with colorful iron-balconied buildings, many of which host temples or meeting rooms for various benevolent societies. If you see wisps of smoke emanating from some them, don't panic—it is just the smoke from incense burning in huge braziers on the balconies. Also as you pass the Hop Sing Tong Building, you might hear the sounds of Sinocast, the Chinese-language radio station which broadcasts from here.

At the corner of Waverly Place and Washington Street, we come to my first reommendation for lunch—Golden Dragon Noodle Shop, 833 Washington Street, open daily.

The Golden Dragon Noodle Shop is a bustling, crowded, quick-order lunch spot which makes no concessions whatsoever to Westerners. But it does dish up incredibly fine Chinese noodle dishes at prices that are positively bargain-basement. And since you are, at this moment, standing right in front of it, now is a convenient time to consider your luncheon choice, even though you may wish to wait a while. My alternate recommendation, Ton Kiang, is a full-fledged restaurant—although by no means a luxurious one!—located a few blocks further on along our tour.

Its cuisine is that of the Hakka people of China, something you will find in few other American cities.

So to help you decide, let's look in the windows of the Golden Dragon and see if it tempts you. From the sidewalk you can see the chefs expertly cleave up orders of golden-brown roast duck. And you might even spot an order of won ton being ladled into a bowl of steaming soup. I consider these won ton to be among the best in town.

So, should the sights through the window be sufficiently tempting, you will require more assistance when inside because most of the waiters speak little or no English and the menu translations tell you little. Let me help.

My favorite dish is Big Dumplings in Supreme Soup. In a bowl of homemade chicken stock float jumbo-sized dumplings, their nearly transparent casings holding a delicious filling of fresh shrimp and vegetables which veritably crunch beneath your bite. The cost of this superb dish is about $2.50! Of course, you may wish to try a bowl of their exemplary won tons, or a combination bowl of won ton and some of those vermicelli-thin noodles. And don't be surprised at the texture of the noodles—they are positively chewable. Far more "al dente" than even Italians are accustomed to. Oh yes, these same won tons are also served with barbecued pork, and the noodles can be ordered with roasted duck. (However, please note that Chinese prefer their fowl and pork on the fatty side and both are served not hot but at room temperature.) Aside from the noodles and won ton in soup, The Golden Dragon also serves Braised Noodles (or dry noodles) with a Hot Meat Sauce. And you've also got to have either Tender Greens or Chinese Broccoli in Oyster Sauce on the side—one portion for every 2 persons in your party. Cooked in under-done Chinese fashion, they burst with flavor and are the perfect accompaniment to the rich noodles. No matter what you decide upon, remember that this place is a noodle shop and that name is not used in vain. You won't find American chop suey. And if you don't drink tea, you won't find anything else other than Coca Cola or Seven-Up in cans, served with a straw. But you will find some of the greatest noodles and won ton outside Hong Kong!

For what awaits you at Ton Kiang, read ahead.

Now, hopefully having made up your mind on where you will lunch, our Chinatown tour must move along. So it's further up Washington Street to take a peek into The Superior Trading Company, 837 Washington. This is a "modern" version of the famed old medicine and herb shops you may have read about. I say "modern" because the countless drawers with their mysterious treasures of roots, herbs and spices are conveniently labeled to help the clerk. In the ancient herb shops, the owners prided themselves on knowing the contents of each drawer and would have died of shame rather than label them.

At 863 Washington is the Tong Hing Pastry Shop. Its claim to fame—Apple pie! Apple pie, that all-American dessert, is a great favorite among the Chinese community, exceeded perhaps only by coconut-custard pies and sponge cakes covered with whipped cream. Chances are you will see all three in this popular shop.

Continuing further up Washington Street, you will come to Stockton Street—turn right. Many years ago, Stockton Street was technically outside the strict confines of Chinatown proper. However, with the ever-increasing influx of visitors to Chinatown, the demand for shops selling "tourist trinkets", like back scratchers and such, began to push the non-tourist oriented shops from Grant Avenue. And the food stores were the first to go, regrouping on a few blocks of Stockton Street where the aromas of their products have made this street more authentically Chinese than parts of Grant Avenue.

Not only have the food stores found haven on Stockton Street but other firms who deal primarily with a Chinese clientele have also relocated here. And perhaps the most important is the Wing Kee Jewelry, 1028 Stockton. Wing Kee is one of the most highly respected purveyors of exquisite jade and this outlet caters primarily to their

Chinese clients by appointment only. (Wing Kee has an even larger outlet, called Tom Wing & Sons, at 190 Post at Grant, which you should visit, if you are looking for fine jade.)

Now, by crossing Stockton Street to the odd-numbered side, you can throw yourself into the throngs of Chinese women as they stock up on fresh produce, fish and poultry. And when it comes to fresh poultry in Chinatown, we also mean live chickens and ducks, sold from trucks parked at the curb. With the reliance of Chinese cooking on the ultimate in fresh ingredients, daily shopping is a necessity. And the examination some of these women put each vegetable or wall-eyed fish through, is remarkable to behold.

Three blocks along Stockton Street, you will reach Broadway. Here turn right one half block to Ton Kiang, 683 Broadway, (421-2015; open daily for lunch and dinner), my alternate luncheon recommendation. Years ago in America the only Chinse cooking you could find was that of the province of Canton. Then came the cooking of Peking, Schezwan, Shanghai, and Hunan. But these are all regional Chinese cooking styles. At Ton Kiang you will experience the cooking of a people—the Hakka. Forced from their northern China homes centuries ago, the Hakka set up colonies in the southern area of China, just like the Cajuns of New Orleans originally were from Acadia in Canada. And like the Cajuns, the Hakka retained many of their original dishes from their ancestral home. And these are what you can delight in at Ton Kiang.

For a starter, you should have their Beef Balls in Spinach Soup. The beef balls are almost spongy in texture, like bouncy liver dumplings and are served in a clear stock which also contains brilliant green spinach leaves. The flavor contrast between the slightly spicy meat balls and the barely cooked spinach is marvelous. They also have Fish Balls, similar to spoon-sized quenelles, served in the same fashion. Next don't miss the Wine-flavored Beef or Chicken—the tender strips of meat tossed with pickled mustard greens and a piquant, uniquely flavored wine-sauce. It has become one of my favorite Chinese dishes!

One of the glories of Hakka cuisine is their inimitable Salt-baked Chicken. This chicken is in no way crisp, as you might think a baked bird would be. But even though the skin is soft, it is totally unlike boiled chicken, more akin to the most succulent *poulet vapeur* of haute cuisine. Here you are given two dipping sauces for the chicken— one is finely minced garlic and ginger in oil, the other a fiery chili sauce. I find I invariably empty both little containers within minutes.

This would be a more than ample lunch for two. But if you are taking your Chinatown tour in a larger group, you try might some seafood dishes, such as their Mixed Seafood Platter. And, of course if it's crab season—mid-November to mid-May—order a crab. Chinese chefs— Hakka, Cantonese, Hunanese, or whatever—can evidentally do no wrong with our Dungenese crab. With this Hakka feast, I enjoy Tsing Tao, the beer from mainland China. Moderate prices for an exciting cuisine you will be hard-pressed to find in most American cities.

Now that you are on Broadway, either having lunched at Ton Kiang or just proceeding along our tour, let me tell you a little about this famed San Francisco street.

Broadway in the few blocks on either side of Ton Kiang has always been one of the city's most colorful streets. Until not too long ago, it was the unofficial boundary between Chinatown and predominately Italian North Beach. On it were located superb late-hour dining spots, like New Joe's. The finest minestrone anywhere was ladled out at Dante's Pool Hall. Pinza and other opera greats ate lustily at the old Fior d'Italia, while you went to the Buon Gusto for salted cod and ceci.

And for years it was the heart of the city's nightlife. Famed Finocchio's, the female impersonator show your grandfather probably saw forty years ago, is still just a few blocks down the street. The original Hungry i was only a few blocks away and the Purple Onion, where an unknown housewife named Phyllis Diller first told of her trials and tribulations in stuffing a turkey, was right down Columbus Avenue at the next corner.

Then in the early '60s Broadway became the supposed hard core of night life—Carol Doda went topless at the Condor on the corner! That seems so tame today, but it ended one era of Broadway and brought in another. To compete, other nightclubs began with topless, then bottomless and on down to live sex acts. And the street went downhill fast! The good restaurants lost their regular customers, who no longer wanted to come to what had become—in the words of an earlier edition of this guide—"mammary lane." So they closed, leaving room for more sleazy clubs, attracting more violence and drugs.

Today, you will find many of the old clubs boarded up and Broadway, especially a block or so nearer the Bay, the once queen of San Francisco nightlife has become a forelorn bag lady. Hopefully, this too is just one of its many phases. I just hope it passes quickly.

Anyhow, right now you need only walk a half block further along Broadway, and turn right to find yourself back on Grant Avenue, Chinatown.

As you head back toward the entrance to Chinatown, where our tour began, you might watch for these shops and spots of special interest:

At 1016, The Ginn Wall Company is a hardware store that also carries a goodly amount of Chinese cooking utensils—woks, steamers, etc. At 903 Grant is Fat Ming Company, a Chinese stationery shop with a marvelous array of greeting cards from Hong Kong. Decorated with traditional Chinese artwork and characters, but with English messages, they make novel and beautiful greetings. You will also note that just about all the cards feature red extensively. Red is the "good luck" color. Thus, brides too wear red, not white, which is the color for mourning.

At the next street corner, Washington, walk downhill a few yards to number 743 to take a look at the marvelously colorful Bank of Canton building—for many years the special telephone exchange for Chinatown.

Our last Chinatown stop, but only if you are shopping for souvenir gifts for children is at 717 Grant, the Chinatown Kite Shop, with kites in the shape of dragons, butterflies, etc., all suspended above a jumble of tourist paraphernalia, such as T-shirts emblazoned with "My Mom and Dad went to San Francisco and all I got was this dumb T-shirt!"

2:00 p.m.   After a morning on your feet, I have planned a "sit-down" afternoon. And that means either a play, musical, symphony, opera or movie—all depending on what day of the week it is, as well as what time of year.

If today is almost any Thursday from mid-September to early June, you might wish to attend an afternoon performance of the famed San Francisco Symphony. Years ago, the matinee audience consisted predominantly of women who made these performances a social habit. Their custom of wearing "correct" gloves once prompted Papa Pierre Monteux, our legendary former symphony conductor, to remark that he could hardly hear the ladies' applause!

The Thursday afternoon concerts often sell out, so you should plan ahead and purchase your seats either at the City Box Office in the Sherman Clay Music Store (392-4400; small service charge) or direct from the Symphony Box Office in the Davies Hall lobby (431-5400; orders can be charged to major credit cards). Symphony tickets can also often be purchased from the various ticket agencies throughout the downtown area and in many hotel lobbies.

Davies Symphony Hall is not one of my favorite concert halls. I find the outside has the appearance of a gigantic bus terminal. Once inside things do not improve much. The architects appear to have had curious ideas about traffic flow, designing the enormous sweeping staircase to empty right into a bottleneck. Inside the auditorium proper, acoustics are variable. And it is a pity, since the Symphony under its new permanent conductor, Herbert Blomstedt, is sounding better than it has in years.

If your musical interests include the lyric world of grand opera, you must already know you are in a world-class city when it comes to that form of theater. The San Francisco Opera, in America second only to the Metropolitan Opera in quantity of performances and second to none in quality, now has a split season. There is a Summer Season which occupies the Opera House from mid-May to early July and the regular, traditional Fall Season which runs from early September to mid-December. However, you may have to search a bit to uncover a ticket to the usually standing-room-only Sunday matinees. Whatever tickets are available can be obtained at the opera box office in the Opera House lobby (864-3330). If they are sold out, you might try one of the independent ticket agencies. Failing this, you can try to unearth a turn-in at the last minute. However, on a sure-fire sellout such as a Pavarotti performance, ticket seekers surround the opera house pleading with arriving patrons for that chance extra ducat which would allow them entry.

Once inside, the Opera House itself is something to see. While it does not possess the elaborate red damask aura of old-fashioned European houses, it is happily not the cold, unfinished concrete and exposed steel of its contemporary sisters. It has spaciousness, comfort, and especially in the upper reaches, fine acoustics. Also, unlike many older theaters, the sight lines are excellent with only a small section of the orchestra seats down front on the extreme sides not having a total view of the stage. (As I mentioned on our First Perfect Day out, the Opera House is a twin structure to the Veterans' Building, across the carriage entrance and garden. Both it and the Opera House served as the site of the signing of the United Nations Charter in April 1945.)

The San Francisco musical comedy scene underwent a major restructuring in the late 1970's. Comet-like, Carole J. Shorenstein burst upon the city. Ms. Shorenstein, whose father just happens to own a great deal of downtown San

Francisco including some of the city's largest theaters, in association with James M. Nederlander launched their "Best of Broadway" series. And the city was alive with the sound of music emanating from not only their three theaters, but from the long-established Civic Light Opera Company, as well. With the demise of the Civic Light Opera, the "Best of Broadway" reigned supreme, importing shows direct from Europe and Broadway, mounting duplicates of some New York hits, and reviving classic musicals of the past. But almost as quickly as they had expanded, things seemed to go sour. The lack of top-notch Broadway shows to import was certainly a major factor.

Therefore, at this moment there is no guarantee that there will be a musical playing at either the Curran, Orpheum, or Golden Gate Theaters. But check the theater section of the Sunday *Examiner & Chronicle.*

San Francisco has always had a strong theatrical tradition dating back to the '49er days. In fact, the thundering of the miners' heavy boots on the bare wooden floors literally could "bring down the house"! Post-World War II days found touring companies and a host of small repertory companies (the most famous being the Actor's Workshop) filling the playbills. Today, the old-time Broadway touring companies which once were the domain of Katherine Cornell, Eva Le Gallienne, Tallulah, and others have all but disappeared.

Today's theater tradition in San Francisco has been kept alive principally by the city's American Conservatory Theater and a bevy of "little theaters". The ACT, as it is known, holds the Geary Theater stage (occasionally overflowing onto that of the smaller Marines' Memorial Theater, too) from early fall to early summer. Its wide-ranging repertory—classics, revivals, contemporary and avant garde offerings—is often presented in a highly original and at times, controversial style. The dominance of local legitimate theater by ACT has also put them in the position of sponsoring what few touring companies there are, which has included England's Old Vic.

Tickets for ACT are available at the Geary Theater (673-6440), one and a half blocks off Union Square, as well as at most ticket agencies.

Many people think that going to a movie is a waste of time while on vacation or on a visit to a new city. I disagree. I think that any full week of strictly sightseeing can become tiring if one doesn't stop once in a while to relax and refuel. And for me, there is no better place to lose myself than in the escape of a darkened movie house where I can become totally occupied by the images on the screen. And if you find a film you have not seen, you might also discover that viewing it at a matinee is not only a pleasant change of pace but a bargain as well, since many cinemas offer reduced prices for their earliest matinee showings.

If there are no theatrical offerings to interest you this afternoon, you might take a very leisurely stroll through one of our museums, again not trying to see everything in all the galleries but just settling down in front of a few favorites in peace and quiet.

5:00 p.m. Having spent your afternoon in a darkened theater, a refreshing contrast might be cocktails from a different vantage point of the city. For this, I recommend the Starlite Roof of the Hotel Sir Francis Drake, conveniently located at Powell and Sutter Streets. This unusually spacious room presents a truly magnificent view of the Bay Area. From its southern and eastern windows, you get a bird's-eye view of the five o'clock commuter-crammed freeways and Bay Bridge approach. You can indeed feel smug as you settle back with no traffic tie-ups to bedevil you and with nothing more critical to contemplate than where to dine this evening. Here are three recommendations to consider.

7:30 p.m. Hayes Street Grill, 320 Hayes Street, San Francisco, (863-5545; dinner served Mondays through Saturdays; lunch served Monday through Friday; reservations for dinner essential usually up to a week in advance). A few years ago "grills" came sprouting up in

San Francisco like mushrooms after a spring rain. What fed this incredible invasion was primarily a change in eating habits—down with blood-red slabs of beef and thick-sauced dishes and up with fresh fish and chicken done over mesquite. The Hayes Street Grill rode into town on this bandwagon and has been its unchallenged leader ever since. It is so popular that if you try to visit it on a night when there are performances at the nearby Opera House or Davies Hall, you must make your reservation exactly one week—to the day!—in advance.

The decor is classic California grill—lean and clean. And the service is cast in the same mold. There is a small basic menu, but the blackboard's daily specials are what most diners follow. For example, it can offer a mind-boggling Black Bean Soup or a Salad of Red and Yellow Beets tossed in walnut oil. Salads, by the way, are never less than sensational here, consisting the the finest greens available anywhere!

For main courses, the fish is always fresh. If you like swordfish, this is the place for you—more moistly tender a fish you could not find. Your choice of two or three sauces are optional gildings. And, if you have never had shark, *Jaws* be damned, these beauties are to be loved. But even though fish occupy the place of honor, do not pass up the meat dishes, especially if it happens to be their Barbecued Baby Back Ribs, a mammoth portion with each rib permeated by a luxurious sauce, which might count apricot preserves amongst its secret ingredients. The Hayes Street is forever receiving "people poll" awards for the best French fries in town. And for once *vox populi* is right!

When it comes to dessert, I hide my eyes from the blackboard's seductive enticements, such as a mesmerizing Pumpkin Custard with Praline Sauce, and remain faithful to my favorite dessert in town—Creme Brulee. Just break through that crackling caramel crust and dip into that immoral creamy custard. Indecent! The wine list offers you fine bottlings from some of California's great but lesser known cellars. A truly great restaurant in a plain brown wrapper. Moderate.

NOTE: For readers who will be attenting meetings, conventions or trade shows at either Brooks Hall or the Civic Auditorium, the Hayes Street Grill is the finest restaurant for lunch in the area. And it's a short three block away.

The House of Prime Rib, 1906 Van Ness at Washington (885-4605; open nightly; no reservations), is the restaurant for people who can not make up their minds about what to order. You see, at the House of Prime Rib, there is no choice—only prime ribs of beef. Oh, there are minor variations as to size of cut and degree of doneness, but that's the extent of it. So if you swimming against the current trendy tide of eschewing beef and are in that roast beef mood, then the House of Prime Rib is an excellent choice. A delicious green salad enhanced by julienne beets and chopped egg, flavored with the special celery-seed accented house dressing, is the perennial opener. Then from their trolley, you select the size cut of roast beef you wish, specifying rare, medium rare or (perish the thought) well done. The quality of their beef is among the best in town and less costly than most comparable versions. Yorkshire pudding, mashed potatoes and creamed spinach are the invariable accompaniments. At extra charge, you can opt for an enormous baked potato in lieu of the mashed (two persons can easily share one order). Desserts are on the simple side: superb Pecan Pie, fresh pineapple and fresh strawberries in season. Aside from savoring the excellent quality food, handsomely prepared, you also will be able to witness the "performance" of a team of waitresses which sets bench marks for efficiency and courtesy. Moderate prices.

Sutter 500, 500 Sutter Street at Powell (362-3346; dinner served nightly except Sunday; lunch served weekdays; reservations advised) is the "stepchild" of Roger Verge, whose Moulin de Mougins in the South of France has garnered three Michelin stars lo these many years. I purposely put a little distance between the founder and the restaurant for while the menu and execution is bona fide nouvelle cuisine a la Verge, the great maitre may not be seen in this kitchen that often, if at all, nowadays.

Physically, the restaurant is divided into two distinct areas: an open, Spartanly appointed cafe in the front and a more intimate, low-ceilinged formal room in the rear. Here the style of decor is quasi-antiseptic, muted, trendy French—the better to showcase the cuisine's brilliant colors and fanciful patterns. But what is critical to me is that most of the offerings scintillate the palate as well as the eye!

For a first course, the Crayfish Mousseline is a delicious puzzlement. I just cannot imagine how Chef Keller can create this cocoon of mousseline into which tiny, exquisitely-sauced crayfish are snuggled. Positively bewitching. The Bay Scallops and Julienne of Smoked Salmon over Linguine is another bravura piece—the pearl-sized scallops are celestial, their pristine pallor contrasting with the darkness of the squid ink-dyed linguini.

The accompaniment to the proverbial fork-tender Medallion of Veal with Spinach and Watercress Cream Sauce is a crepe of pasta along with a miniature garden of baby vegetables. If it is a light mint sauce for the Filet of Lamb and Sweetbreads, then for the Roasted Breast of Duck, it's a delicate ginger-scented one that caresses the correctly rare slices. And so it goes—one culinary fantasy follows another. Desserts vary each night and sometimes in accomplishment with one another. Wines are rather pricey. But for anyone even remotely interested in the word of nouvelle cuisine as preached by one of its original high priests and executed by a equally awesome disciple, a visit to Sutter 500 is essential. Oh yes, its location one block from Union Square makes it an ideal, albeit expensive, shopping-day lunch spot.

10:00 p.m.   Again, it has been a long day—with even more walking planned for tomorrow. So my suggestion now is to head back to your hotel, sprawl out on your bed and perhaps catch a rerun of "Streets of San Francisco" or any of the dozens of films which have used this most photogenic of all American cities as their backdrop. And since you are such a San Francisco hand by now, try and spot the geographic errors, such as having a police chase begin at the Golden Gate Bridge Plaza and end two seconds later atop Nob Hill. Now, you and I both know that's not quite possible. Right? Pleasant dreams.

Your Fifth Perfect Day Schedule

9:00 a.m. Only a light breakfast, because we will be having an early lunch.

10:00 a.m. A walking tour of Japantown, where yesterday and tomorrow meet in the flutter of cherry blossoms along a peaceful mall, and in the glare and blare of electronics equipment in a modern trade center.

12:00 noon Lunch at an authentic Japanese restaurant where both novice and Nipponphile can savor the finest tempura and gyoza in town.

1:45 p.m. A journey through San Francisco's past, strolling down the tree-shaded streets of famed Pacific Heights, one of the poshest urban neighborhoods in America.

3:00 p.m. Union Street where today's chic shops are housed on a yesterday street. Late afternoon cocktails in one of its famed "watering spots."

8:00 p.m. If you wish to stay in the Union Street area for dinner, you can revel in refined Russian cuisine. Or discover American cuisine—yes, not "cooking"—carried to the ultimate in one of the city's most talked-about, elegant hotel dining rooms. Or enjoy a taste of New York with the greatest steak or lobster in town!

10:30 p.m. Still on the go? Well, how about going to San Francisco's own *Beach Blanket Babylon*?

The Fifth Day of Your

One Perfect Week in San Francisco

9:00 a.m. Today will be your chance to experience more of the feel of this marvelous city—through the soles of your feet! It will be a day that can be savored only by a good deal of walking—ambling down a stone-paved Japanese mall, strolling through the quiet tree-shaded streets of luxurious Pacific Heights, browsing in and out of the crazy-quilt warren of shops along Union Street. In all, today will be a kaleidoscope of sights, uniquely San Francisco.

Of all the itineraries in this book, today's was the most difficult to map out. In leading you from one area to another, I wanted to avoid any strenuous climbs—a near-impossible feat in hilly San Francisco. But by following my directions, you can effortlessly take the day in stride. There will be no need for a car, for we will travel by foot and public transportation. Be sure you have a good supply of change, because you need the correct fare on the city's buses. The other requisite is a good pair of walking shoes.

10:00 a.m. After a light breakfast, walk to Union Square and, on the corner of Powell and Geary, board a #38 Geary bus (not the limited, but the regular #38). Ask the driver to call out Webster Street for you. If he remembers, your destination should be reached in about fifteen minutes. On leaving the bus, cross Webster Street (note the street sign is also written in Japanese characters), turn right, and enter the doors of 1581 Webster.

In the 1950's, when Japanese trade with the United States began to burgeon and tourism across the Pacific took on the aspects of a commute run, Japanese business interests drew up plans for a culture-and-trade center that would not only showcase Japanese products, but cement stronger cultural ties with San Francisco. Discussions, plans and the inevitable delays seemed to go on without end. Finally, the three-block long complex, which you have just entered, materialized. Whether the idea was too grandiose or the site, appropriately located in San Francisco's "Japantown," was too distant from downtown shopping and foot traffic, the success the planners envisioned has never been achieved. For example, the enormous Kabuki Theater, which was launched with glittering imported Japanese reviews, bit the dust shortly after opening. And while the Miyako Hotel, which towers over the east end of the center, enjoys capacity business, the trade center itself does not seem to attract too much interest. I suspect the lack of great success can be attributed also to the center's obvious touristy air, with bazaar-style shops and such come-on's as "pearls in every oyster" attractions. Nevertheless, the center is well worth a brief walk-through and you can start by climbing the stairs directly in front of you.

On reaching the upper level, proceed to the left across the covered bridge which usually contains some fine examples of Japanese art on loan from the Avery Brundage Collection, housed in Golden Gate Park. Directly before you on the east side of the bridge you will find one of my favorite stops in the center, the Ikenobo Ikebana Society Headquarters. Ikebana is the art of arranging flowers. And here, in the showcase windows, you can feast your eyes on a few outstanding examples. Practitioners of this delicate art form can achieve more grace and beauty with one iris, a single leaf and a bent twig, than I have ever seen anybody do with two dozen long-stem roses! If you are interested in learning more about the age-old art and traditions of ikebana, here is your opportunity.

However, another feast for the eye, if not for the pocketbook, is the Murata Pearls displayed right across the way. Only a few doors away from the serene, frozen poetry of ikebana, you will come in contact with the jazzy, garish glitter of the dozens of Japanese TV sets currently on the market. At the end of the long arcade is the official Japan Information Service, run by the Consulate General of Japan. If you contemplate ever journeying to the fabled city of Kyoto, here is where you should stop to garner all the information you will need.

Immediately on passing the information center, you will exit from the west wing of the center onto the Peace Plaza, with the Peace Pagoda rising above its reflecting pool. Here you might wish to sit a moment and look out over the western half of the city. There is little need to bother with the east wing of the center since it only houses less of the same.

Directly across Post Street from the Peace Plaza is the latest addition to Japantown, one that I believe represents a more beautiful way to attract visitors to the area. For unlike the huge concrete dinosaur of the center, the shopping mall you see before you is far more evocative of what most Westerners like to think of as Japan. True, the center is more representative of today's concrete-and-steel Tokyo. But we have enough concrete and steel in our own cities, and travelers search for something else.

In 1907, when the Japanese colony resettled here in the "Western Addition" after the '06 fire, the buildings had no oriental flair. Unlike Chinatown, which was devastated in the fire and rebuilt with nods to Chinese architectural styles, Japantown consisted of Victorian wood houses dating from the late 19th century. The fire never reached this area; by dynamiting Van Ness Avenue, it was confined to what we know as the downtown area and Nob Hill. When these old wood buildings began to deteriorate beyond repair, nondescript, more modern dwellings and shops replaced them. Then, a few years ago, instead of waiting for the old structures on this block of Buchanan Street to tumble one by one, they were razed and a Japanese village street of yesteryear rose in their place. Down the center of the wide mall curves a serpentine pattern of stones, connecting two fountains made of stone and iron. The cherry blossom trees and azaleas bloom in the spring and if you are here at that time of year, you can watch their blossoms flutter earthward as you sit on one of the benches. The shops bordering the mall sell today's Japanese electronic products and the like, but they also contain some fine examples of folk art and kimonos. It is a lovely place to enjoy a sunny San Francisco day.

Before you take in the mall, however, cross Post Street and turn right along the street's north side. There are a couple of shops you might enjoy browsing through. For example, on the corner is Soko Hardware. Here you will find not only the usual hardware items but also all manner of supplies, pots and planters for bonsai growers. Further down the street at number 1656 Post is the Uoki Sakai Company.In this grocery store, you can view the finest and freshest of vegetables arranged by hands which must have been trained in ikebana! And if you think you have sampled just about every known product of our earth, just glance through the displays of gobo, daikon and other roots and greens, all part of Japanese gardening and cuisine.

Now, retrace your steps to the mall. As you amble up the slight incline, you may wish to check the dates on the posters announcing festivals in the community. If one is happening during your stay, a return visit might be in order to witness some time-honored traditions. For example, during the last week of April, Japantown bursts into cherry-blossom festivities with the Sakuramatsuri Festival. Colorfully garbed in kimonos and other classic Japanese costumes, the participants parade before a backdrop of stately Victorian houses—another uniquely San Francisco happening. But for right now, continue on up the mall to Sanko at 1758 Buchanan Street. Inside you will discover a treasure trove of modern Japanese wares— sake sets, rice bowls, tea pots, etc., which make lovely, yet relatively inexpensive, gifts for friends back home.

When you reach the top of the mall, cross Sutter Street to the American Fish Market. Since one of the glories of Japanese cuisine is sashimi (raw fish), the freshness of sea products is of infinite importance. And the American Fish

Company carries a wide variety of tuna, favored for sashimi, as well as octopus and other denizens of the deep. In the far left corner is a tiny sushi counter, where cold rice and seaweed are used as the major ingredients to create a style of snack food, uniquely Japanese.

On leaving the American Fish Company, be sure to take a look at the two buildings almost directly across Sutter Street (Nos. 1771-1777 and 1782-1787). Both were constructed in the in the 1880's as "double houses" with each house later turned into a duplex. They are fine examples of Victorian San Francisco architecture. (For readers with more than a cursory interest in architecture, I heartily recommend: *Here Today: San Francisco's Architectural Heritage,* sponsored by the Junior League of San Francisco, Inc. and published by Chronicle Books.)

Now, walk back down the right-hand side of the mall, browsing through some of the shops, such as the Paper Tree at 1743. In this stationery store you will find the papers and instructions necessary for origami, the Japanese art of paper folding, which make for unusual gifts. And further down the mall you might investigate the N. B. Kimono Store at number 1715.

At the bottom of the mall, turn right a few feet and you will find yourself at one of the finest Japanese restaurants in San Francisco—Sanppo, 1702 Post Street (346-3486; closed Mondays; no credit cards). And since it is open for lunch—which is what you should be considering about now—just walk right in.

12:00 noon   When you enter Sanppo, you could be entering any one of a thousand small restaurants in Japan. To say the place is clean is slanderous—it is immaculate. The waitresses dart around each other as though performing a ballet choreographed for swallows. And the cooking is superb, especially the tempura which is peerless in town. To the uninitiated, tempura is but one style of Japanese cooking, one in which a whole range of seafoods and vegetables can be covered with a light batter and then quickly deep-fried. It sounds simple enough but to insure the correct gossamer lightness and to avoid any signs of greasiness, a chef must have a built-in stopwatch. You will discover Sanppo's excellent tempura for yourself when a plate of shrimp, sweet potato slices and other fresh vegetables, all encased in their light batter-cocoons, are placed before you.

In fact, you might wish to split an order of tempura as a first course and then proceed to other dishes, such as the gyoza. Almost every ethnic variety of cooking has some manner of meat in pastry—Italy has its ravioli, Russia its pelmeni, China its kuo-tieh, and Japan its gyoza. Gyoza is ground pork touched with garlic, enveloped in a paper-thin dough, and fried on one side only. Delicious! In salmon season, do not miss the magic a great Japanese chef can perform on this often mishandled fish. And speaking of fish, Sanppo is also an ideal place for those who admire sashimi (raw fish), because if you are fully acquainted with this great delicacy, you will appreciate Sanppo's masterful presentation, a delight to both eye and palate. Sanppo is an ideal restaurant for both the newcomer to Japanese cuisine as well as the Nipponphile, at moderate prices.

1:00 p.m.   When you leave Sanppo, turn right and walk two blocks to Fillmore Street. As you near Fillmore, it is a good time for me to point out another attraction of the Trade & Cultural Center which is traditionally Japanese, but of which you cannot avail yourself right this moment— a shiatsu massage. Located in the far west end of the center is Kabuki Hot Spring (922-6000), a Japanese massage center. Here you can bask in the tension-releasing euphoria of a hot tub and sauna, followed by the shiatsu massage. This method concentrates on pressure points in the body rather than on the overall body-caressing usually associated with American or European massages. And you will find no hanky-panky at Kabuki—try the downtown area for that!

At Fillmore Street, turn left one block to the nearest bus stop, on the Geary Street overpass. Board a #22 bus, asking the driver to announce Jackson Street. Actually, it would be great fun to walk these nine blocks, but it probably would take its toll on your energies which you will need for later on. So sit back and relax while you observe the incredible cultural mix along the sidewalk—for on this section of Fillmore Street no one ethnic group has proprietary rights. You will see Japanese restaurants (the last outposts of Japantown), soul-food kitchens (the furthest extensions of lower Fillmore's black ghetto), Chinese lunch counters, antique-junk dealers, recycled clothes shops, amidst chic boutiques and restaurants on this revitalized street. However, by the time your bus reaches Jackson Street, the neighborhood suddenly becomes less commercial—for you are on the threshold of Pacific Heights, one of the poshest urban neighborhoods in America.

1:45 p.m.   Leave the bus at Jackson Street and walk one short block further to Pacific Avenue. Turn left on Pacific and you find yourself on a tree-shaded street, light-years removed from the atmosphere of only a few short blocks away. Here, the residential architecture varies greatly in style from the Classical Revival beauties at numbers 2418 and 2420 to the false-fronted Italianate of the Leale House at number 2475. Queen Anne, Baroque, and English are all to be seen. But more than lessons in architecture, these grand homes represent the wealth and taste of the founding families of San Francisco who built most of them in the closing years of the last century, high on these heights commanding a view of the entrance to the Bay, just as feudal lords built their castles on equally strategic points along the Rhine and Danube. You can share this eagle's-nest view by glancing down Steiner Street to the Bay and the hills beyond.

Five blocks along Pacific, turn right down Broderick Street to Broadway. Yes, this is the same street which houses the roaring, neon-bedecked topless joints of North Beach. But the loudest sounds you may hear in this part of town probably will belong to the electric clocks of the silent Rolls-Royces as they glide by. Some of the most grandiose houses in San Francisco will be found on the next two blocks, to your left. For example, just look at the one at 2901! One block beyond, Broadway ends at a gate to the Presidio. So here, turn right and walk down the stairs alongside the Presidio fence to Vallejo, one block below.

I can never descend this flight of stairs without being taken back in time to a more leisurely era when these houses were constructed, when nannies sunned their charges on the park-like landings, when the domed Palace of Fine Arts you see before you was just one building in a fairy-tale city. Now, empty aluminum cans shock the greenery, and street lamps stand blind and broken. At Vallejo Street, turn right and continue two blocks to Broderick; then downhill two blocks to Union Street.

3:00 p.m.   At this point, you have a decision to make. If you feel that the pre-lunch walk combined with the one-hour tour through Pacific Heights have proven too much for your stamina, you can simply board a #45 bus and ride back to Union Square right in the heart of downtown. Or, if you are still game—and I hope you are—you can turn right and proceed along Union Street, up the slight rise and over the top.

Years ago, Union Street was a rather sedate shopping area, filled mostly with little antique stores run by quiet-spoken gentlefolk. Then, some "with-it" boutiques began intermingling with the antiques. In their wake came the singles bars, the "watering spots" which cater to the young swingers in search of each other. So today, this six-block stretch of Union is a wild smattering of everything—fun and funky, garish and glamorous, sedate and insane. And you can pick and choose as your tastes dictate.

However, before your senses are assailed by all this, you might wish a calm moment to rest your feet by passing through the lych gate into the courtyard of St. Mary the Virgin's Episcopal Church at the corner of Union and Steiner. In this oasis, the silence is broken only by the splashing of waters from an artesian well into a fountain basin.

Now, on to Union Street. I will not provide you with a door-to-door guide for two reasons. First of all, the shops seem to have an unpredictable life span; and secondly, the range of tastes along this street is so wide that it would be difficult to cover the entire spectrum.

On the corner of Fillmore and Union, you should take a short side trip down Fillmore Street to visit some especially outstanding shops. For example, Mark Harrington, 3041 Fillmore, features the finest in crystal and all manner of stemware. And further down Fillmore, in the next block at number 3131, is T. Z. Shiota, one of the city's most respected oriental art shops.

Heading back up to Union Street, on the even-numbered side, you come across (at number 3028) Shibata's, another excellent oriental art dealer.

Back up at Union Street, turn left and you will find yourself in front of one of the fanciest 7-11 Stores you will ever see. It now occupies the site formerly the home of Jurgensen's, purveyor of fresh caviar and other toothsome delicacies. I think that is rather indicative of what has been happening to Union Street.

Before I leave you to browse on your own, I'd like to give you a few more tips. First of all, don't keep your eyes riveted only to Union Street's tempting shop windows. Look up at the buildings themselves. While the display may be of the latest hair styles or haute couturier fashions, the buildings, such as number 1980, are charming old relics, many dating from the late 1800's. Also keep in mind that whenever you tire, you can always catch the #45 bus which takes you back to the Union Square area. The last thing I want to mention is one of the most unusual houses in San Francisco, the Octagon House. Located right off Union at 2645 Gough (five blocks from Fillmore), this eight-sided structure dates from 1861 and its unusual shape was due to the then popular belief that the octagon represented good luck. It now houses a museum and is owned by the National Society of Colonial Dames.

Naturally, if thirst overcomes you along your Union

jaunt, you can easily stop in at one of the numerous "watering holes" such as the popular Perry's at number 1944 and, in the meantime, decide on where you will dine this evening.

8:00 p.m. For dinner tonight, I will let you choose between three restaurants—all are excellent in their own way. The first is located in the Union Street neighborhood, and would be especially suitable for those who wish to linger here until evening and enjoy a modest-priced but delicious Russian dinner. The second is situated downtown, right off Union Square, and is one of the city's most exciting (and expensive!) restaurants, where the ultimate in American cuisine is proudly presented. The third is a taste of New York with the greatest steak and lobster in town! It's all up to you. . . .

Archil, 3011 Steiner off Union (921-2141; dinner served Tuesday through Saturday) is the cozy, intimate, modestly-priced hideaway everyone hopes to discover, but seldom does. And when you do, the food is usually miserable. But that is not the case here. At Archil's the cuisine is refined Russian—not elegant and costly caviared blinis, etc., but the standard Russian culinary repertory, executed with awesome finesse and served handsomely in a genteel atmosphere of candlelit congeniality.

Although Archil's offers complete dinners (at remarkably modest prices!), I must always opt for an a la carte order of their delectable Herring. If you fancy this fish, do not miss it here. Then comes a tureen of hot Borscht, a brilliant beet/tomato-red soup, chock-full of vegetables including plenty of the requisite cabbage. Ladle on some sour cream and just try to resist emptying the tureen!

I always request that their lovely Romaine salad be served after my main course, and proceed on to perhaps their ideal Golubtsy, beef-stuffed cabbage rolls, or their exquisite Kotlety Pozharsky, ground chicken cutlets of infinite lightness ashimmer in drawn butter. For something more novel, try the Chicken Tamara—a poached chicken treated to a sprightly Georgian (USSR not USA!) sauce of finely ground walnuts, touched with cilantro.

Served with all main courses is a fine pilaf and a fresh vegetable. Of course, no Russian restaurant could exist without Beef Stroganoff and Archil's is excellent; as is their Shalik.

After my salad, I favor the Kisel, a type of Russian jello preparation, this one made from red wine. The Coffee Cheese Cake is decidedly un-Russian but excellent. There is an adequate wine list at comparably moderate prices to accompany this remarkably refined Russian cuisine. Positively a bargain!

Campton Place, 340 Stockton Street, (771-5112; breakfast, lunch and dinner served daily; reservations imperative) totally disproves two previously long-held culinary beliefs. One: that hotel food in the United States is only next to airline food in unmitigated mediocrity. Two: that America has no real cuisine, just "cooking." For here in a refurbished downtown hotel's elegant dining room, all done in peaches-and-cream, you will find American cuisine raised to heights, equal to the greatest gastronomic peaks of France or anywhere else for that matter. Resident Chef Brad Ogden searches out the finest typical American ingredients, then coaxes them into a brilliant style of cuisine that is still proudly American. Does he succeed with every dish? Of course not! No one does. But even his lesser achievements are more exciting to me than some of the humdrum successes of non-creative, by-rote chefs.

Take for example, the warm Corn Bread that welcomes every diner. Come on now, have you ever tasted better? Just about to crumble as they aproach your mouth. And inside, the chef's conceit of including whole, moist kernels of corn, like raisins. The Fried Catfish—what's more American than catfish?—is ethereal, tempura-like in execution and the accompanying ginger-lime sauce the ultimate dip. Caesar Salad is also American, but this plate of innocently young baby Romaine leaves caressed by an peerless dressing and dotted with tiny fresh croutons is light-years removed from the usual heavily doused, crudely coarse Ceasars. The New England Clam Chowder borders on overreach; it is almost too elegantized with its tiny flecks of bacon and bits of celery in a creamy rather than milky stock. But the Souffle of Black Chanterelles is other-worldly in its airiness. A Soup of Roasted Tomatoes and Eggplant holds a float of scallion cream.

For main courses, the Grilled Loin of Lamb with Nicoise Olive Butter cannot be improved on. But what is that mysterious puree beneath the tiny chops? Parsnip touched with perhaps cinammon, thus fashioning it into an imitation apple sauce! On the plate are the tiniest of carrots and red Swiss chard. The ideally grilled Veal Chop is smothered in sauteed black chanterelles, while on the side are barely cooked infant spinach leaves along with a tiny wild-rice souffle. The stuff of which dreams are made!

The Brownie Pie shows that there is only so much you can do to some typically rich, typically American chocolate desserts. But the Coconut Pot de Creme totally captivates. Also in the spirit of the American palate is a coterie of after-dinner coffee concoctions, madly mixing in liqueurs and cream.

The check arrives. It's delivered by one of the young serving persons, whom I find as refreshing as the cuisine. They are not the obsequious old retainers of formal French dining rooms. But they are knowledgeable and efficient. Including a bottle or two from an adequate wine list, the check is probably more than you had reckoned. But if you really love fine dining, Campton Place is unique and thus priceless.

Palm, 586 Bush Street at Stockton, (981-1222; Open nightly for dinner; lunch served Monday through Friday; reservations advised) *is not* a great restaurant. But it *is* a great steak and lobster house! And if while in San Francisco you crave either, then without question Palm should be your destination.

Let's face it: San Francisco was never a great place for steak. OK, we did have some good steak houses, such as the now closed Grison's. But they could never really compare to the great steak places of New York. First of all, it was a question of the quality of the beef. Western beef simply cannot hold a candle to mid-West beef. Secondly, it's the aging: Palm ages its beef for two weeks in New York, then ships it to its eleven restaurants, located throughout America. There, the beef is aged for yet another week! What aging does is break down the meat's fiber, tenderizing it. Combine that tenderness with the superlative flavor of the finest mid-West beef, and you will find the Palm New York Strip Steak to be *the* single best steak in San Francisco.

And then there is the lobster. The American lobster is found only in the Atlantic, primarily off Nova Scotia and Maine. Therefore, prior to the jet age, these beauties were simply unavailable in San Francisco. And even when jets made it possible to fly them in live, most restaurants only brought in "chicken lobsters," those weighing 1¼ to 1½ pounds. That gave a true lobster-lover slim pickings. And unlike most other critters, a lobster's meat does not toughen with size. So when you are properly bibbed up and sit down in front of one of Palm's 4 or 5 pounders, it's feasting time! Again, as with the New York Steak, it is the finest—if not the only!—lobster to enjoy in San Francisco!

As with Gotham's great steak places, everything at Palm is strictly a la carte. That means your steak will arrive on a plate barren of even a parsley sprig. But a side order of their superlative French Fried Onions can be split for two, as can their Hashed Brown Potatoes. (We split that one for four! Oh yes, and they will even split their steaks and lobster.) But what else do you need in a great steak or lobster dinner?

And that is just about all I can readily recommend at Palm, with the exception of their authentic New York Cheesecake, which, to me, is *the* only true American cheesecake. Because if you decide on the String Bean and Onion Salad, you might find that the beans appear totally raw, although that fact is not mentioned on the menu, and the onions too thickly sliced. The Clams Oreganato can be coolish with a gelatinous veil over the oregano-flavored liquid which surrounds them. And while the Clams on the Half Shell can be fine, the Linguini with White Clam Sauce might be shamelessly vapid and overcooked. And surely in San Francisco, Palm can find a better source to replace its current lamentably poor French bread!

But when it comes to steaks and lobster and their basic gustatory partners, Palm is truly oustanding. And for the first time since it closed, I no longer miss Grison's. Palm, we're glad you came to town! Very expensive.

10:30 p.m. Well, if after gallivanting all over Japantown, Pacific Heights and Union Street, you are not bushed, you might enjoy taking in a performance of San Francisco's perrenial and ever-popular musical revue, *Beach Blanket Babylon,* which plays at the Club Fugazi, 678 Green Street in North Beach. On certain nights, this very funny uniquely San Francisco company puts on a show that should be beginning just about now.

Your Sixth Perfect Day Schedule

9:00 a.m. Easy on breakfast. It is going to be a long fun- and food-filled day as we tour the beautiful and historic wine country north of San Francisco.

9:30 a.m. Drive across the majestic Golden Gate Bridge to Sonoma and the Valley of the Moon.

10:30 a.m. Stroll around Sonoma's town square, visiting handicraft shops and viewing buildings dating from California's colorful past.

12:00 noon Your options for lunch today include dining at a superb French country restaurant or picnicking at one of the state's loveliest and most historic wineries.

2:00 p.m. Your tour of the wine country continues as you leave the Valley of the Moon and cross the hills into the famed Napa Valley.

3:45 p.m. Your final winery visit is the most spectacular of all as an aerial tramway carries you to a hilltop complex overlooking the valley below.

6:00 p.m. On the way back to San Francisco, you have your choice of dining in a uniquely San Francisco institution located in Marin County, or at my favorite Cantonese restaurant, or at a tiny fish market-restaurant only frequented by locals.

The Sixth Day of Your

One Perfect Week in San Francisco

NOTE: Later on in this guide there is a recommended three-day trip to the Napa Valley, which covers some of the same area as this one-day outing. You may wish to refer to it, when making your plans for this shorter visit.

9:00 a.m. Weather permitting, this full-day excursion can be the highlight of your San Francisco stay. (Even though it may be foggy in downtown San Francisco, chances are it will be sunny in the wine region.) Featured are the scenic beauties of one of the world's richest wine-producing regions along with delectable accents on food and fine California wines, as well as glimpses of California's past. However, it is a long day, so I advise starting now, perhaps fortified by a very light breakfast at your hotel.

9:30 a.m. Drive out to Van Ness Avenue, a thoroughfare with which by now you should be well acquainted, and head north toward Lombard Street which leads onto the Golden Gate Bridge. Approximately 20 miles along Highway 101 on the Marin County side, turn off onto Highway 37 (marked "Vallejo, Napa"). Seven and a half miles later, turn left onto Highway 121 (marked "Sonoma, Napa"), continuing for another 6½ miles. Here, watch for signs leading to Sonoma, turning right and then left 1 mile later onto Highway 12. Proceeding up Highway 12 (now called Broadway), you will soon make out directly ahead the old Sonoma City Hall. However, before you approach the town square, look to the left corner of Broadway and Andreaux where you will spot a yellow building with a sign announcing, Au Relais. Tuck the location of this restaurant in the back of your mind someplace. Now, on arriving at the town square, turn right, locate the nearest free parking space, and begin your walking tour counter-clockwise around the square.

10:30 a.m.   Sonoma is a charming little town steeped in early California history. It is the home of the last California mission, the location of the Bear Flag Republic, and the still-intact home of General Vallejo. Luckily, before all visible vestiges of this colorful period of California's past had been eradicated in a post-World War II remodeling fervor, a movement was launched to preserve some of the historic buildings. Therefore, as you stroll around the square, it will not be too difficult to sense what this town was like in the 19th century. However, not all the delights of Sonoma are of yesteryear. As in 1850 when people fled Gold Rush-crazed San Francisco for the calm of Sonoma's lovely valley, young artisans today are drawn to this unhassled, friendly town where they are keepers of small shops in which you will find a wide variety of their handcrafted work.

But before I begin my browsing in any of these stores, I always stop by the Sonoma French Bakery, 470 First Street, next door to the movie theater. Don't be too surprised to find this tiny bakery jam-packed with a line extending onto the sidewalk. Why? Well, as any of those patient patrons will verify, this bakery turns out the finest sourdough French bread in the world! Now, I know that is quite a statement. But it just happens to be true. And how they do it, no one seems to know. Their other baked goods are quite ordinary. But, the French bread . . . *c'est magnifique!* (By the way, since it is unavailable in San Francisco, any and all city friends would warmly welcome a loaf.)

Continue up First Street. On the far corner, you will find the old mission where, during the fall harvest, the grapes for the new vintage are blessed in a religious ceremony that has been conducted on this spot for years. Now, turn left along Spain Street, the northern perimeter of the square. Here, you will find the barracks which once housed General Vallejo's troops; plus a restored hotel from a later date. Along this street you will also come upon the Sonoma Cheese Factory, 2 West Spain (open daily).

But before you go inside, let me ask what you would like to do for lunch . . . picnic at a historic winery or dine in a beautiful French country restaurant (remember Au Relais, the yellow building)? While it may be too early to actually lunch, you should decide now since Au Relais accepts no reservations at lunch for parties less than six, and it can become crowded during the mid-summer months. If a picnic tempts you, let me say that the Sonoma Cheese Factory has just about everything you will need, including some of that fabulous French bread from the Sonoma Bakery. As is only natural in a cheese factory, great emphasis is placed upon cheese and you will find over 100 varieties. Be sure to sample some of their originals—Sonoma Cheddar and Sonoma Jack. You also can buy beer here but who would think of drinking that alien brew in California's beautiful wine country! Wine is the thing and of course, the Cheese Factory has that, too. However, if you are in a picnic mood, I think you'd have more fun if you waited and purchased your wine at the Buena Vista Winery—your luncheon spot—after tasting a few of their offerings.

If you still are not sure about what you want to do for lunch, don't flip a coin. Park yourself on the sidewalk bench and read ahead.

Au Relais, 691 Broadway, Sonoma (707-996-1031; open daily for lunch and dinner), is a dream of a country restaurant—lovely art-nouveau decor, fleet-footed service, superbly prepared dishes from an inspired and highly original menu. And even though the weather in Sonoma can be pretty hot in the summer (how do you think those plump grapes ripen?), I would not let the heat dampen my appetite or discourage me from taking full advantage of their menu. To start, there is a haunting cold Cucumber and Spinach Soup, an ideal summer refresher. Or you may wish a sunny Salad Nicoise, that South of France melange of tomatoes, beans, tuna, anchovies, etc.

moistened with olive oil. Enjoy it with some of that sensational French bread, which Au Relais purchases from the nearby Sonoma Bakery.

Although in France, the great classic Cassoulet—an incomparable stewed medley of beans, sausage, meats and fowl—is generally restricted to winter menus, Au Relais happily dishes up its own somewhat spicier version year round. Or, if you wish a meatless main course, you cannot go wrong with the Fettuccini al pesto.

But before opting for either of these main courses, inquire if there is any fresh fish on hand. For example, the poached salmon in a light butter sauce, perhaps studded with a few mushrooms, is breathtaking.

If summertime visitors to Northern California miss out on our wintertime-only crab, they are somewhat compensated by our superb summer salmon. And Au Relais is a fine place to relish it. As an added bonus, most main courses here are amply garnished with fresh vegetables cooked ideally al dente.

Even when it comes to desserts, Au Relais maintains its independence from the humdrum by creating novelties such as Beignets, those elegant crullers associated in the U.S. with breakfast in New Orleans. But Au Relais dresses theirs up with a lovely apricot sauce! Yet, their Tarte Tatin is one of the finest you will encounter locally. This warm-from-the-oven, upside-down, caramelized apple tart is heaped high with whipped cream for a hedonist's delight. A tough decision!

Probably because the great wine growers of the area are Au Relais habitues, the wine list reads like a "What's What" of California cellars, featuring some bottles from those new limited-production "boutique wineries." All in all, truly delightful dining experience, made especially memorable if you can lunch *al fresco* on the flower-bedecked patio. And moderate prices!

Now, with the "where to lunch" question resolved, you can go inside the Sonoma Cheese Factory and shop around a bit and/or head down Broadway to Au Relais if reading about all that luscious food has made you hungry. First, though, while you are in the area, you may wish to visit General Vallejo's home, part of the State Department of Parks (small admission). In this Gothic Revival house, you will view rooms just as they were in the late 1800's, replete with Victorian furnishings brought around the Horn. On the hillside above the house is a lovely shaded artesian-fed reservoir, which gave the property its name, Lachryma Montis—or "tears of the mountain."

If you are going picnicking and have your provisions in hand, drive to the southeast corner of the square and continue on Napa Street heading east until you cross some railroad tracks (about 1 mile), turning left immediately thereafter.

In a few minutes you will find yourself in an idyllic setting which is not only an active winery with tree-shaded tables outside for your luncheon comfort, but a historic spot as well. It was here that General Vallejo first planted grapes in 1832. But it was not until the arrival of a Hungarian nobleman, Count Agoston Haraszthy, that the Buena Vista was established as one of the first wineries in California. After searching the West for over a decade in order to locate a suitable climate in which the grape-cuttings of his native Hungary would flourish, the Count discovered the Sonoma area or, as the Indians called it, the Valley of the Moon. Here he settled, striking up a close friendship-rivalry with General Vallejo (who was a proud amateur vintner) and by 1857, bottled his first pressings.

Because of his pioneering work in what is now one of California's most famous industries, Haraszthy has been officially recognized as "The Father of California Viticulture." The vine-covered stone building on your right dates from this early period of California's wine history. Stepping into its cool interior, you can take a short self-guided wine tour, which takes you back into the barrel-lined mountainside cellars, dug by Chinese laborers over a century ago. In the tasting room, you may sample some of the Buena Vista's current output.

No matter if you decided to lunch "al fresco" here or inside Au Relais' charming restaurant, the Buena Vista Winery is a "must-see."

2:00 p.m.   Time to tear yourself away from either Au Relais' Gallic creations or your picnic spread and wend your way back to Sonoma's town square, where you should continue out Napa Street to the west this time. Following the Highway 12 markers toward Santa Rosa, you will soon pass through small towns such as Boyes Springs, Fetters Springs and Agua Caliente, names harkening back to when this area supported many spas, fed by hot mineral springs from the nearby mountains. Six and a half miles after turning off Napa Street, keep a careful eye open for a sign indicating "Trinity Road— Oakville." Turn right here and almost instantly, you will find yourself climbing a ridge of mountains with over-the-shoulder views of the Valley of the Moon behind you. Remain on the Oakville Grade and you will abruptly top the crest. Before you, in sweeping panorama, lies the fertile Napa Valley. Visitors who have never toured wine-producing areas are often shocked to discover that in late fall, grape leaves turn into the flaming red, deep orange, and purple of New England's fall foliage. Should this be the time of your visit, this view is all the more awesome.

Proceed down the grade to Highway 29, turn left and you are in the very heart of the great Napa Valley. If you are at all cognizant of California wines, the next several miles north will be mind-boggling. Concentrated along this road are some of the most famous names in California wine-making—Beaulieu, Inglenook, Robert Mondavi, Beringer, Charles Krug—all with tasting rooms! In order to weed out the Sunday imbiber from the more serious wine taster-purchaser, many wineries have been forced to insist visitors take a tour prior to entering the tasting room. Therefore, the number of wineries you visit and how much wine you sample is up to you. But watch the clock. Our last scheduled winery is Sterling Vineyards, 1 mile south of Calistoga off Highway 29. Another one of our "must see's," it closes at 4:30 p.m. which means you should arrive there about 4:00 p.m.

3:45 p.m. Well, time to head further north to the far end of the Napa Valley and Sterling Vineyards. After passing the Napa Valley State Park on your left, start watching for a cluster of white buildings on a hilltop to your right. Once in sight, you may think that somehow the stark white structures of an Aegean Island have been magically transported to a California landscape. (Camera buffs take note: You will be leaving the winery via a different route. Therefore, this unique view will not come again.) Just when you think you have missed the turnoff, you will see a sign indicating "Dunaweal Lane, to Sterling Vineyards" and others directing you to the visitors' parking area. Here, at the hill's base, is an aerial tramway which will silently carry you up to the winery for a $5.00 per person charge. It is worth every cent. For at the summit, you can conduct yourself through one of the most beautiful wineries in the state. Actually, the interior is comparable to a contemporary museum with ancient and modern art depicting all phases of wine-making. Each step of the process is clearly explained and the actual machinery is visible.

Yet, not even this impressive tour can compete with the vista of the surrounding lush valley. I have intentionally scheduled your arrival here late in the day when most of the visitors have departed. At this more quiet time, the winery takes on a monastic air. And when the many bells—originally from St. Dunstan's Church in London—peel out from their towers, it is a moment to remember.

Naturally, wine tastings are available in a handsome lounge or on a sunny patio. Out-of-staters can be somewhat frustrated if they become attached to Sterling wines as they are difficult to locate in most liquor stores. Sterling prefers to reserve much of their output for purchases at the winery and for diners in finer restaurants.

6:00 p.m. Well, time to leave the tranquility of this

marvelous white aerie, and press on. So glide back to the valley floor via the tramway and exit from the winery, this time to the right. Soon, another right will head you back down the Napa Valley, not on Highway 29 but rather on the lesser traveled Silverado Trail.

Since all the wineries are now closed, I prefer to use the less trafficked Silverado Trail for this portion of my return to San Francisco. Being a less commerical route, you are closer to the beauty of the vineyards around you.

Simply continue down the Silverado Trail until it dead-ends at Trancas Street in Napa. Turn right for 2 miles, then left onto Highway 29 (marked "Vallejo"). Now follow Highway 121 signs which will lead you into Highway 37. Highway 37 will lead you directly to Highway 101 south to San Francisco, which is the route we started north on this morning.

While traveling back to San Francisco, you might wish to consider having dinner at one of three restaurants, purposely included in today's schedule for four very important reasons: all offer superb food; all are easily accessible from the route you must take to reach downtown San Francisco (no need to change your clothes, casual attire perfectly acceptable); none accept reservations, therefore you will not have to worry about arriving at a set time; and all three offer a simplicity which would ideally cap this long day.

Marin Joe's, 1585 Casa Buena Drive off Highway 101, Corte Madera (924-2081; open nightly for dinner and for lunch weekdays), is one of a breed of restaurants indigenous to San Francisco. To any resident, a "Joe's" restaurant immediately means an open charcoal grill, a heavily Italian-accented menu with equal emphasis on steaks and chops, and counter as well as booth service. San Francisco still boasts several Joe's, yet today, the mantle of "top Joe's" rests securely on the shoulders of this Marin County roadside operation. Here, frozen vegetables are shunned (except for an occasional appearance in the mixed-vegetable garnish) and shortcuts, such as powdered stock concentrates in the minestrone, are abhorred. What you find is good wholesome, down-to-earth cooking, expertly done by a team of chefs who work with dazzling elan. Their performance is best witnessed from a ringside counter seat.

Start with a cup or bowl of Marin Joe's fine minestrone, followed by either a Rib Steak (that old-fashioned, deliciously juicy cut so seldom found on today's menus) or their extra-thick Lamb Chops (medium rare, of course). Naturally, be certain you specify your steak or chops be charcoal broiled. The pastas are also quite fine but you must request that they be cooked to order, al dente, for which you pay a slight premium.

Side orders of vegetables play important roles in any Joe's meal, especially at Marin Joe's where they are fresh. Therefore, I always ask that the mixed vegetables which come with the meat courses be replaced (at a slight charge) by either Swiss chard, Italian beans, zucchini or spinach. All these vegetables have been parboiled in advance. However, each order is sauteed to order in olive oil with a touch of garlic, arriving at your table piping hot and delicious.

One dish that every Joe's and only a Joe's features is the Joe's Special. Legend has it that late one night many years ago, a group of regulars arrived at a Joe's to find the kitchen's food supply almost depleted. All the chef could stir up were some eggs, ground beef, onions and leftover parboiled spinach. Well, stir them up he did, scrambling them into a concoction that is neither scrambled eggs nor omelette but strictly San Franciscan! On request, Marin Joe's will add fresh sliced mushrooms for an elegant touch.

Desserts are almost non-existent except for a sensational Zabaione, that frothy Italian delight of whipped eggs and Marsala wine. I prefer Marin Joe's version to any in San Francisco's far more deluxe and expensive restaurants. But then, quality takes center stage here, not elaborate service or fancified decor. And there are countless San Franciscans willing to drive across the Golden Gate and encounter a possible wait for a table, just to indulge in the finest example of this uniquely San Francisco style of dining. Moderate prices.

To reach Marin Joe's, as you drive south towards San Francisco on Highway 101, after San Rafael start watching for a turnoff to the right marked "Paradise Dr.—Tamalpais Dr." Take this exit and proceed to the second stoplight, keeping to the far left. Turn left onto Casa Buena which runs parallel to the freeway. Marin Joe's is on the right. After dinner, all you need do to reach San Francisco is continue south on Casa Buena and in a minute, you will be able to re-enter the freeway, heading to the Golden Gate Bridge and your hotel.

Another dinner suggestion is: Mike's Chinese Cuisine, 5145 Geary Boulevard at 16th Avenue (752-0120; dinners served nightly except Tuesdays). Let me state without equivocation—Mike's is not only a great Cantonese restaurant, but after searching for years I have not found its equal in San Francisco. Mike's is also a rather unusual one. Unlike the majority of its Cantonese counterparts who offer a minimum of 150 different selections, Mike's menu is very brief. And while all too many Chinatown places continue to add more and more inexpensive ingredients, such as huge chunks of celery, onion and bamboo, to stretch dishes and keep costs down, Mike's does not hesitate in raising prices while keeping the quality pristine. Furthermore, whereas the rotation of chefs in large establishments, especially those open for lunch and dinner, often makes Chinese dining a variation of Russian roulette, at Mike's, Mike is personally in the kitchen just about every night and therefore, the consistency is practically unfailing.

Mike's style of clear, unencumbered cooking is apparent in my perennial first course, an ethereal Mustard Green Soup—sparkling clear broth, brilliantly green underdone mustard greens, tender filets of pork and a shred of ginger. The delicate sweetness of the superb stock and tender pork contrasted with the quasi-bitterness of the mustard greens represents, to me, the quintessence of Cantonese cuisine My second course is usually the

Chicken Salad, that compelling mixture of shredded chicken, lettuce, coriander and onions. Then, if you fancy sweet and sour pork, meet the San Francisco champion: Sweet and Sour Pork de Luxe. Cubes of tender pork, batter dipped and fried to insure the proper outer crispness, are bathed in a luxuriant sauce rich with translucent pieces of preserved melon, pineapple cubes, and gingery delicacies. The Paper Wrapped Chicken is another favorite, while the Crystal Shrimp (quickly stir-fried so they all but explode in your mouth) are brilliant. If, like me, you simply cannot get enough of the refreshing clean flavors of Chinese vegetables, then try the Tenderloin with Chinese Greens, or the Beef with Sugar Pea Pods.

End your dinner, as most Chinese would, with a stellar Steamed Rock Cod, its silk-smooth sweet flakes gently flavored by ginger, onion, coriander and soy sauce. That should ring down the curtain on a perfect Cantonese dinner! And should you return here next year, you would find the exact same undulled freshness, expert flavor balance, and stylistic simplicity. No, it hasn't been a dream: it was just dinner at Mike's. Moderate prices.

How to reach Mike's? Cross the Golden Gate Bridge into San Francisco. A few hundred yards past the toll plaza, curve to the right following the signs to 19th Avenue and Golden Gate Park which, via a tunnel, will whisk you through the Presidio. At the fourth stoplight (Geary Street), turn right for two blocks and you will find Mike's on the left-hand side of the street. After dining, all you need do is head down Geary in the opposite direction from which you arrived. Geary will take you directly downtown.

My third recommendation makes its debut in this edition of the guide, but not because it is new. La Rocca's Oyster Bar, 3519 California Street (387-4100; lunch and dinner served daily except Sundays) is a fish market first and a restaurant second. Seating only about three dozen patrons, located far from downtown San Francisco and closing promptly at 8 p.m., it is not the type of place visitors would seek out. That is, unless they wanted the ultimate in plain but absolutely fresh fish.

Yet, "Where do I get really good fish?" is the question I am most frequently asked. When I reply that restaurants such as the Hayes Street Grill, Jack's and others serve superb fish, most visitors seem disappointed that I have not named a fish restaurant *per se*. Well, the problem is that I do not like most traditional sea food houses in San Francisco. I gave up on Wharf places years ago, and in this edition I dropped my former favorite, Tadich Grill, after watching the kitchen slide further into carelessness.

Now, don't misunderstand me. I am speaking of my personal preference. Tadich still enjoys enormous popularity, and not just with visitors. But I can no longer recognize its Boston Clam Chowder as even a remotely reasonable facsimile and the deep-fried scallops could easily be confused with McDonald's Chicken McNuggets. But no longer able to recommend Tadich, how could I publish a book on San Francisco, a supposed great seafood city, without a seafood house? And that is why I have decided to reveal La Rocca's.

Even without a single out-of-towner, La Rocca's is perennially crowded, a short line forming by the counter nightly. The help, wearing Levis, knows just about everybody by name. There are no individual menus, but what is in is posted on a huge sign behind the counter, along with the current prices, which can suprise the first-timer. Yes, you can find abalone here—at $27 a portion! The kitchen is the size of a broom closet, so nothing fancy is prepared. The container for the Boston Clam Chowder is in the dining area. And let's start right there.

La Rocca's serves my favorite Boston Clam Chowder because they understand that with this dish, less is better. And that means, you will not find in it all kinds of extraneous ingredients and thickeners—just clams, potatoes, and onions in a milky clam stock. Most San Francisco restaurants mistakenly believe that clam chowder is some kind of porridge. It ain't.

Then there is the crab, when it's in season. Here you

can get fresh crab served in the shell, because that is the way La Rocca sells it to go. You will not find that in many non-Wharf fish restaurants. What most use is crab which has been "processed" by having been treated to a light saline solution, which helps preserve it but which also removes some of its innate nut-like flavor.

And then there is the fish itself. What is listed on that board is guaranteed fresh. The finest in petrale sole (one of the Pacific's finest fish), halibut, swordfish, salmon, seabass, snapper and whatever else happens to be in the catch. At times La Rocca's will also have imported fresh scallops with their roe intact, brought in from New Zealand.

As for how the fish is prepared, you have your choice—broiled or grilled. Oh yes, they will occasionally serve a sturdy fish in a Milanese breading, meaning a coating of breadcrumbs, grated cheese and parsley. But that's as far afield as they will go. No fancy preparations; no casserole combinations; not even a French fried potato! But what you will receive will be the finest in fresh fish, expertly prepared. Take for example, a halibut steak I had there. It was snow white, ideally cooked to a moist flakiness, with the most dulcet flavor you can imagine, slightly touched with garlic and oil. Served with it was the best tartar sauce in the city and sliced zucchini. That was it. And that was as good as halibut gets.

Frankly, I don't rightly know if La Rocca has desserts. I don't think I have ever seen anyone order one. Oh yes, they do have Italian biscotti that you can order with a glass of Cinzano. But I usually end my meal with a superb cappuccino. So now you know my favorite fish restaurant in town.

To reach La Rocca's on your return from the wine country, after reaching the San Francisco side of the Golden Gate Bridge, follow the signs to 19th Avenue and Golden Gate Park. On exiting a short tunnel, turn right at the first light (Lake Street), then immediately left onto 14th Avenue for one block to California Street. Another left on California Street and you will be at La Rocca's in about 20 very short blocks. After dinner, just continue on California Street which will take you back downtown.

10:30 p.m.   Well, whether you dined at Marin Joe's, Mike's Chinese Cuisine, or La Rocca's you now should be back at your hotel probably just as bushed as I am. However, if you're not (bushed, that is), all I can say is any carousing you want to do after a day like this will have to be done on your own! Good night. See you tomorrow.

Your Seventh Perfect Day Schedule

9:00 a.m. Time only for a quick coffee before you launch your last day in San Francisco.

10:45 a.m. Either tie up all those last-day loose ends or relax aboard a cruise ship and tour the Bay, seeing San Francisco from an exciting, different perspective.

12:00 noon Enjoy a buffet high atop a Nob Hill tower with a 360-degree view of the Bay or lunch in a crowded waterfront "find" with a clientele as varied as the menu!

2:00 p.m. It's a free afternoon. Enjoy it by revisiting and resavoring your favorite corner of San Francisco. Or take a hike!

6:30 p.m. With the city at your feet, sip a farewell cocktail in one of our high-in-the-sky rooms.

8:00 p.m. A final elegant dinner at either the city's most venerable dining room, or in a bastion of French cuisine seldom discovered by tourists, or experience an old San Francisco culinary tradition on Pier 39.

10:30 p.m. If you are heading home tomorrow morning, or are setting out on one of the exciting side trips detailed in Part Two of this book, you had better call it an evening. So until we meet in San Francisco again, *au revoir, auf Wiedersehen, arrivederci*—so long.

The Seventh Day of Your

One Perfect Week in San Francisco

9:00 a.m. Good morning! Well, this could be your last full day in San Francisco. Therefore, I purposely have framed a very loose format for you today. I know that whenever I enjoy a week or more in any one city, I invariably find that on my last day, there are many loose ends to take care of, such as returning the rental car, picking up purchases held at stores, firing off a few last postcards, etc. Also, there are favored places to revisit, to resavor before leaving. Or some new ones to discover. And for you, today is that last day to fit it all in.

So since it is going to be a busy day—with a good-sized lunch—why don't we just get moving after a quick cup of coffee?

For those of you who have tied up all those loose ends and wish to experience another facet of San Francisco this morning, I am not about to abandon you. Why not enjoy your last perfect morning in San Francisco on San Francisco Bay?

10:45 a.m. At Pier 43½ hard by Fisherman's Wharf you will come upon a ship of the Red & White Fleet (546-2810) ready to take you aboard for a 45-minute cruise of the Bay. These cruise ships depart as early as 10:45 a.m. daily, and at 30- to 45-minute intervals thereafter, depending on the time of year. (The ships of the Red & White Fleet are also available for charter. Each ship can accomodate from 50 to 500 passengers and can depart from one of several San Francisco, East Bay and Marin County docks. For further information on chartering call 546-2829.)

On board and under way, you will turn westward toward the Golden Gate. From either the warmth of the enclosed lower deck or from the breeze-swept top deck, you can watch the San Francisco skyline pass in review. First, Fisherman's Wharf with Russian Hill in the background; then Fort Mason and the Marina with its row of luxury homes overlooking the yacht harbor. A taped narration, happily bereft of those lame puns and stale jokes which afflict most tour talks, will call your attention to points of interest ashore. You will be acquainted with many of the landmarks, such as the Palace of Fine Arts and Fort Point, having already visited them earlier in your stay. But the Bay cruise places them in a different, overall perspective, set against the backdrop of the city's hills and, hopefully, a brilliant blue sky. Soon, your ship will timidly poke its prow under the Golden Gate Bridge, gracefully arching high overhead, and hastily turn back from the choppy waters of the entrance to the smoother Bay itself. Within a few minutes, you will be gliding by Alcatraz, now deserted except for bands of curious visitors traipsing through the vacant cell blocks. On the port side, you will see Treasure Island, site of the 1939 World's Fair and now a U.S. Navy base. If some of the buildings appear a bit grandiose for a naval installation, it is just that they are remnants of the Fair's exotic architecture.

And then it's back to Fisherman's Wharf with the exciting skyline of downtown San Francisco towering high above in the background. It is a marvelously impressive sight.

12:00 noon By now you will have docked at Fisherman's Wharf. And unless you wish to revisit The Cannery or Ghirardelli Square, I suggest you head to your luncheon spot.

My two recommendations are as different as can be! One is not noted for its cuisine, but rather for its 360-degree view of San Francisco. The other is located in a funky waterfront jazz joint (by night), but offers a wonderful eclectic menu to an equally wonderful mix of San Franciscans. Let's start with it.

The Cooking Company at Pier 23, The Embarcadero (362-5125; open Monday through Friday for lunch only;

Sunday brunch served; reservations advised; no credit cards) is very typically San Francisco. Without any formal publicity whatsoever, word got out that great luncheons were to be had in this tiny dilapidated old jazz joint on the waterfront. And suddenly Pier 23 was "in". Not like the media-hyped, trendy places which put forth a "theme" with little regard to cuisine, and then close as the theme becomes shopworn. But 'in" because its eclectic menu— with a noticeable leaning toward Indonesia—is truly exciting. And the place is great fun, too! Here preppies, opera board matrons and waterfront types rub elbows at tiny tables. Oh yes, there is a view of the Bay, but it is only visible through the windows high above the bar. But here is what you can expect to see before you on your plate.

The Chinese Chicken Salad is only remotely related to the ones we know from places like Mike's Chinese Cuisine. Here the good-sized shreds of chicken meat have been tossed with slivers of red cabbage and lots of sesame seed, and bound with a slightly spicy Indonesian peanut sauce, rendering it much richer and creamier than the true Chinese version.

The Fresh Grilled Prawns with Nuoc Mam Sauce are flawlessly sweet and tender; the dipping sauce hauntingly fragrant with mint and tamarind. The rest of the plate is a United Nations assemblage—typically American mashed potatoes, an ideally seasoned French ratatouille, and underdone, reed-thin asparagus spears that are Chinese in execution. A Pork Satay with Peanut sauce is much more forthrightly Indonesian and delicious: the thin little filets as tender as one could hope for, anxious to be dipped into the somewhat spicy pureed peanut sauce.

For dessert, a rum-saturated Chocolate Pound Cake and an equally intoxicated Vanilla version are sensational in their open homemade goodness. Some interesting but not too costly California wines are available by the glass as well as the bottle. You pay the surprisingly modest bill with cash—no plastic. And when you walk out onto the Embarcadero afterwards and gaze up at Telegraph Hill in front of you and the Bay at your back, you know you can only be in San Francisco.

If you took my recommendation for a morning Bay cruise, you can easily walk to Pier 23 from Pier 43½. Hopefully it is a sunny day, and this part of the Embarcadero is delightful.

On your way you will soon pass Pier 39. Many visitors—and certainly most San Franciscans—who are reading this book might be wondering why I have never mentioned Pier 39 before. Certainly it has become one of the city's major "tourist attractions." The answer is simple: I, personally, do not like it. To me, Pier 39 is everything that San Francisco is not. Walking through it, I receive the impression that Pier 39 is a forced collection of too many shops and far too many restaurants, all crammed together to maximize the "income per square foot ratio."

Unlike Ghirardelli Square, which has an innate charm inherited from its previous chocolate-factory incarnation, Pier 39 is too up-front commercial, too blatantly hard sell, too "touristy." While I often enjoy a stroll through Ghirardelli Square, just to savor the place without any intention of entering a single shop, I would never think of doing this at Pier 39. To me, although it is architecturally appealing, it has no intrinsic charm, character or grace—attributes long considered synonymous with San Francisco.

However, as the French are wont to say, *chacun a son gout*—each to his own taste. Therefore, you may enjoy the quasi-carnival atmosphere of Pier 39. Its enormous carousel and other "midway" attractions are certainly appealing to youngsters, especially. And many visitors to the pier have no doubt found it great fun. But, as with a visit to Alcatraz, it's just not my cup of tea.

This section of the waterfront has been developed into a lovely landscaped water's edge promenade. Yet, a little further along at Pier 35, you might find a huge ocean-going liner loading up for a four o'clock sailing to the Orient, Alaska, or wherever. And fog or shine, you will be passed by dozens of joggers who use the Embarcadero as their exercise course.

However, if you wish an eagle's eye view of the entire Bay as an exciting backdrop for your lunch, then my second recommendation would be just the aerie for you.

The Crown Room, Fairmont Hotel, Mason and California Streets (772-5131; buffet lunch served Monday through Saturday), is perched on the very top of the Fairmont Hotel Tower high atop Nob Hill. Yet aside from its awesome view it offers luncheon goers probably the most impressive buffet in town.

Actually, buffets can be the bane of any food critic's life. It has become painfully apparent that the vast majority of chefs who prepare buffets are seriously infected by the "dazzle them with quantity" virus and are totally impervious to the "it's quality, not quantity" antidote. The most noticeable talent these so-called chefs display is their ability to operate a can opener, as evidenced by endless bowls of canned fruit, assorted olives and artless tuna salads. I, therefore, usually avoid buffets like the plague! Luckily for you, however, the Crown Room buffet is a noteworthy exception. First of all, this buffet is extremely high on fresh, top-quality ingredients. Gleaming bowls of fresh papaya, pineapple, berries in season, etc., greet you. Secondly, there is no skimping on the more costly foods, copious platters of pates, delicate bay shrimp and even poached fresh salmon, when in season, are often part of the lavish display.

And when the more ubiquitous buffet fare, such as pickled beets, cucumber salad, chicken salad, etc., are used, each is touched with creativity by intriguing vinaigrettes or sauces, or mixed in palate-pleasing combinations which offer a parade of delightful flavors and textures. On the other hand, the Crown Room's chef is only slightly more successful than most buffet builders when it comes to presenting hot selections. I suppose it is asking too much of them to come up with hot dishes capable of withstanding the steam table's debilitating environment. Even though some of these hot dishes can appear above average, I approach them with skepticism, concentrating on the superior cold offerings. Pastries are nice, but not Oscar winning. All in all, the excellence and variety of the buffet's cold course, combined with the breathtaking view, make the Crown Room a rare and delightful experience. Expensive.

Of course, if you decide to lunch at the Crown Room the best way to reach it from the Pier 43½ Bay Cruise dock is by cable car. You'll find the Fisherman's Wharf terminal for the Powell Street line just a few blocks from the pier at Bay and Taylor Streets. So hop on for your last ride and simply hop off at the Fairmont Hotel. Also, be sure to take the outside elevator up to the Crown Room. You'll love the way the Bay panorama unfolds as you climb higher and higher.

2:00 p.m. I have nothing really specific planned for you this afternoon; as the tour brochures would say, it is a "free afternoon." Perhaps you want to fill it by revisiting your favorite San Francisco places, by strolling through Chinatown once again, by dropping in at that museum which you just didn't have enough time for, by sitting contentedly in Golden Gate Park and soaking in its beauty and freedom.

But if you would like a couple more suggestions, I do have two totally diverse ones.

One is to experience the ultimate in urban environments by strolling through the Embarcadero Center. Here, in an area just west of the Ferry Building, on the site of what was once San Francisco's produce markets, loom the flat, grey, sky-reaching towers of what many natives originally called with great disdain Manhattan West, the Embarcadero Center. However, I believe that secretly many San Franciscans rather relished watching these steel and concrete monoliths rise, imparting to the city's skyline a far more dramatic profile. During the day, the Center is ant-hill alive with thousands of office workers who do not even have to touch street level (walk-overs interconnect the massive structures) to shop, lunch or sun in the flower-festooned open spaces. But at night, the

Center is almost deserted, even though its many restaurants lure diners with the welcome of free indoor parking, etc. On a moonlit night, with its giant steel sculptures agleam, you can get the eerie impression you have been transported to some mysteriously abandoned world of tomorrow.

While browsing through the mall-like Center, you might wish to do a bit more shopping with an eye towards finding something to take home with you as a suitable memento of your San Francisco stay . . . something that will recapture for you the look and feel of the city. Why not drop into a bookstore and ask for a copy of *Above San Francisco, Volume II*, published by Cameron & Company? This breathtaking volume of color photographs presents San Francisco in all her glory as seen by a swooping gull or jet pilot. Dazzlingly photographed from above, in a clarity which rivals that rare light of the Aegean Islands, this is San Francisco as we who live here like to think of her . . . and as we hope you will remember her.

My other suggestion is to see San Francisco from as dramatic a viewpoint as those in Robert Cameron's book. No, I am not suggesting you take a helicopter ride over the Bay, although they are available, but rather that you take a hike in the hills of Marin.

I do not know another city on earth that offers those who like hiking a greater opportunity to do so within just a few minutes from the heart of the metropolitan area. But in San Francisco, it's a snap! And don't forget your camera. We're off to a photographer's paradise.

On Van Ness Avenue, at either Geary, Sutter, Clay or Union Street, you can catch a Golden Gate Transit bus (for information call 332-6600) that will in about 15 minutes take you across the Golden Gate Bridge and into Marin County. (On boarding the bus, make certain it stops at Spencer Avenue above Sausalito; as of this moment the #20, #50 and #80 all do so.)

On leaving the bus at Spencer Avenue continue along the frontage road for a few hundred feet, until you reach an underpass on your left. Walk through this underpass and you will see immediately ahead trail markers indicating the trail head. The initial 15 minutes is up a rather steep trail, part staircase, cut into the hillside. But take your time. At each turning, new views of the Bay open up, while the eucalyptus groves through which you pass always sustain some wildflowers. At the top, turn left. When you reach a paved road, a sign will indicate a trail on the right, which you should follow in the direction of San Francisco. Here the going is easy, along an almost level trail that cuts across the hillside covered with a host of wildflowers. You might even spot some grazing deer. Off on your right is the Pacific Ocean. And then as you round first one bend then another, the vast vista of San Francisco emerges, piece by piece.

If you hike out far enough, you will come to one of the great dream spots favored by both amateur and commercial photographers ever since the Golden Gate Bridge was built. For you will actually be above the tops of the bridge's towers and beyond them lies the entire city of San Francisco, stretching from Bay to Ocean Beach. I know of no comparable view—anywhere!

Once you have your fill of this magnificent spectacle, simply retrace your steps, back down the trail-stairs to the highway. And right there, within a few yards of the last step, is the passenger shelter from where you can board a San Francisco-bound bus (departures at thirty-minute intervals).

Crossing the Golden Gate for the last time, you will have time to think back on your visit. And perhaps, if you have fallen in love with her as much as the writers of these words, you might consider just "What is San Francisco?" I hope you won't mind, if I add my thoughts.

Countless columnists and authors have mulled over the question for years and the library is packed with their varied conclusions. There are even entire books devoted to the subject. To follow in the wake of such illustrious company is daring, but I do not feel this book would be complete without my attempt.

To understand the lure and charm of San Francisco, we

must first destroy a myth. That myth is the notion that San Francisco is a "second New York." Nothing could be further from the truth. San Francisco and New York are completely different. For sheer facilities, art museums, theaters, restaurants, and every other diversion, there is no city in America to compete with New York. However, San Francisco, while offering a somewhat lesser variety of these diversions, does make them more accessible to everyone. And when you add to that its charm, its less frantic atmosphere, its bayside beauty and its generally benign weather, then San Francisco has no peer.

It is impossible to answer the question, "What is San Francisco?" without falling into a kind of flowery, self-conscious prose which defeats its own purpose. I have never read a good description of San Francisco. And not wishing to follow failure with failure, I will attempt to answer the question, "What is San Francisco?" by simply summing up the city's outstanding points.

San Francisco is in the unique and fortunate position of offering its residents and visitors many of the facilities of a great metropolis without forcing them to sacrifice their natural love of greenery and fresh air. It is a city of views, of shiny leaves, of sunsets, of water, of green earth. In New York City, for instance, it is quite possible to live in Brooklyn or Queens and to travel back and forth to work in Manhattan by subway and never, except by chance, see any expanse of water or groves of trees. Not so in San Francisco.

The very heart of the shopping district on Market Street provides one with a clear view of Twin Peaks. From the top of elegant Nob Hill the East Bay and rural Marin County can be easily seen. And in just moments you can be out in the country, amidst wildflowers and deer.

And as major cities go, San Francisco is relatively uncrowded. On the downtown hub's busiest day, the Friday after Thanksgiving Day, the crowds are no more dense than on an average day along New York's Fifth Avenue.

And perhaps it is this less frantic environment with

fewer annoyances than are encountered in other large metropolitan areas, that allows San Franciscans to lighten up, to not take themselves too seriously! Although civic pride is never in short supply, we like nothing better than to kid our city, its officials, and most of all—ourselves.

I've always believed that part of the lightness of San Francisco, its easier life style, may be a partial reflection of the city's actual physical color. For basically San Francisco is a white city. That becomes most obvious when you view it from the vantage point of the Marin headlands. Not only its skyscrapers but most of its homes are light in color, and, particularly on a sunny day, have a just-scrubbed look about them which continually gives the city a fresh youthful character.

And I believe that since all the above traits contribute to a less hectic, less harassed life, San Francicans have the time to be more courteous. We take almost a civic pride in our day-to-day courtesy. There are exceptions, of course. But by and large, restaurant personnel, clerks, even bus drivers, and especially the wonderful breed of cable-car gripmen dispense courteous treatment freely to the public. Simply purchasing a loaf of bread in a busy bakery will often find kind words or small talk exchanged between customer and clerk. And visitors from large Eastern cities are always amazed at the courteous treatment by taxi drivers, famous elsewhere for their rudeness.

Will it last? Will the uniqueness and individuality of San Francisco last? In a way, yes. Nevertheless, every day brings change. Real estate interests have physically altered the face of downtown San Francisco to almost beyond recognition from a few decades ago. For example, it was not that long ago when Bush Street gave you a full view of the Bay. Now you look into a wall of glass and steel. Every day small, individual shops and restaurants give up the ghost, because skyrocketing rents force them out. And usually they are replaced by the commonplace corporate.

So while the city which I hope you enjoyed this week

is not at all the same as it was even fifteen years ago, I believe the intangible San Francisco is changing far more slowly. Because whether we be native or newcomer, we feel we are San Franciscans and are a part of something very, very special.

6:30 p.m. Where will it be for cocktails this evening? Perhaps a return to the Top of the Mark to watch it grow dark, or an other go around of the Equinox Room, or maybe you would like to sample a different room-with-a-view, the one high atop the St. Francis Hotel Tower called Victor's. A high-powered outside elevator propels you above Union Square in a matter of seconds. Once seated in one of the semi-secluded alcoves, you can gaze out over the entire downtown area, the Bay and the East Bay hills beyond. Whichever view room you choose, the city lying at your feet will now, I hope, seem a very familiar place, filled with a great many memories to cherish.

8:00 p.m. If it was difficult for me to select from among all our great restaurants the ones to offer you on your First Perfect Day, the choice is equally challenging for tonight. Not only do I want to provide you with fine cuisine, but also the appropriate atmosphere for that true San Francisco finale. In addition, while the three I have decided upon range in price from moderate to expensive, their greatest contrast lies in their approaches to dining out in San Francisco.

Swiss Louis, Pier 39 (421-2913; open daily for lunch and dinner; reservations), is a holdover from a once-great San Francisco dining tradition—the "complete Italian dinner".

At one time, true "complete dinners" were a great and highly respected San Francisco dining style, and North Beach restaurants rivaled one another in laying before diners stupendous spreads of outstanding quality. As time passed, some of the exponents of this family style of dining went highbrow—with more fancified, strictly a la carte menus. Others now cling only to a sparse skeleton of this former glorious tradition, padding out their main courses with a vapid soup and limp salad. But Swiss Louis has keep the "complete dinner" alive in the grand manner.

Your first course will be a mammoth tray of Italian hors d'oeuvres—prosciutto, mortadella, copa, salame, black and green olives, celery, pickled mushrooms, marinated artichoke bottoms, pepperoni, and ceci . . . a meal in itself! This spread is equally impressive in quality as well as quantity! Plenty of fresh French bread is on hand; and served almost simultaneously is a provocative green salad enhanced by Bay shrimp and tossed with a sprightly dressing which crosses a Louis (no relation) dressing with a vinaigrette. This is followed by a homemade minestrone-like soup, filled with fresh vegetables.

In selecting a main course, I usually opt for the "Broiled Chicken". If we used the actual Italian name for this dish, Pollo Schiacciato, it would sound less prosaic but taste just as good. Here a half chicken is compressed in a heavy iron framework and then broiled. This process results in a more uniformly crisped skin and a juicier interior. The Sauteed Prawns are deftly handled and bask in a lively capers-wine-lemon sauce, far removed from most batter-laden presentations. Even some of the steaks are treated to unusual "house" preparations. All main courses are garnished by flavorful fresh vegetables.

Unfortunately, Swiss Louis has done away with the traditional finale to this San Francisco-style complete dinner—an abundant basket of fresh fruit and nuts. After a copious meal like this, the cleansing acidity of a fresh orange or the natural sweetness of an apple once filled the bill ideally. Today, their overly sweet Chocolate Mousse seems out of place. Nevertheless, given the size and excellent quality of this dinner—with a handsome view of the Bay as a bonus—at a remarkably moderate price, Swiss Louis can be regarded as a "best buy".

Jack's, 615 Sacramento Street near Montgomery (986-9854; open nightly for dinner and for lunch Monday through Friday; reservations imperative), is a cherished

San Francisco institution of well over a hundred years. The great-grandchildren of the Bay Area's finest old families today dine at their ancestral tables. But do not expect anything elaborate at Jack's. Its decor is men's room lighting and plastic palms; its service can be brusque (I once wrote that you had to refuse the first table and send back the wine to gain the attention of your waiter); its noise level can be high. However, its cuisine is honest, unfrilly basic French.

The menu changes daily but if today happens to be a Saturday, do not miss the ambrosial sorrel soup. Their simple unsauced fish, such as the infinitely fragile Sand Dabs, are outstanding. Their rack of lamb, crispy outer crust and meltingly pink within, is always excellent and served with potatoes boulangere—an unbeatable combination. Also try a side order of their deep-fried eggplant or zucchini. For dessert: any fresh berries or melon in season; or their incomparable French Pancakes, not the fancily flamed ones known as Suzettes, but rather simple little crepes. The coffee, served in cafeteria-style crockery, is just about as bad as anywhere in town. Nevertheless, if I were forced into exile and had to leave my beloved San Francisco, my last meal would be the above described feast—not only because it is so superb, but also because it is served at Jack's. Expensive and no credit cards.

Le Castel, 3235 Sacramento Street (921-7115; dinners served nightly except Sunday; reservations a must), is regarded as one of San Francisco's finest French restaurants. Yet, relatively few visitors find their way to this stylishly redone residence out near Presidio Avenue. Why? Well, Le Castel has eschewed the kind of tourist-enticing publicity ploys practiced by so many more well-known restaurants. Instead, owner Fritz Frankel during the past few years has quietly developed a limited yet remarkably adventuresome menu, happily marrying nouvelle to classic French cuisine in a style reminiscent of Tailliavant in Paris. With it he has earned for Le Castel the loyalty of a large and devoted local clientele, among whom I am happy to include myself.

Where to begin? Well, if you relish brains, you cannot afford to miss the Calf's Brains in Black Butter. Their custardy texture is perfectly preserved and their dulcet flavor is ideally framed by the nut-like browned butter and the accent of capers. Yet, the Oyster and Spinach Bisque is green satin. Or a magnificent fish mousse—of fresh halibut on one evening—wearing a spinach cap and surrounded by an aristocratic *beurre blanc.* But also, pay attention to daily specials. For you can reap such rewards as a Confit of Duck served over coarse-cut, cooked cabbage, scented with carraway and juniper berries.

For main courses, the Stuffed Squab salutes the Haeberlin brothers, those three-starred chefs of Alsace. The sprightly seasoned stuffing is flawless and its slightly pungent bed of cabbage reminds us that Alsace borders upon sauerkraut-relishing Germany. Or if you cannot get enough of our California artichokes, try the Medaillons of Veal Murat, fork-tender veal cloaked in sliced artichoke bottoms. Yet, the lamb is unbeatable. The choice is dazzling and it's yours!

If you wish a light dessert after such an abundance of riches, their custards and Bavarian creams, festive with all manner of fresh fruits and berries, provide just the right light touch as a finale.

The wine list at Le Castel shows as much understanding and daring as the menu. For example, on one evening I found a Tualaten Pinot Noir, 1980, from Oregon's Williamette Valley (yes, Oregon!) to be sensational. But don't ask for it, it's probably all gone by now. But do ask Mr. Frankel for his suggestions on both wines and cuisine.

For even though its subdued atmosphere, correct service and exciting menu has made Le Castel the favored dining spot for a large segment San Francisco's most serious diners, Mr. Frankel is the consummate host and will graciously take the time to assist anyone who wishes his input in constructing a perfect dinner. Indeed, should you take my and his recommendations, you might come away saying that with Le Castel I have indeed saved the very best for the last.

10:30 p.m.   The time has come to say good-bye or at least *au revoir.* If you are remaining for a longer period than a week, the balance of this book will help you enjoy this extra time. But if you have to catch that next plane home, let me say I hope you have enjoyed our One Perfect Week in San Francisco together. I know I have enjoyed bringing it to you.

PART TWO

Two-, Three- and Four-Day Trips

Around San Francisco

A Two- or Three-Day Trip

Up the Coast to Mendocino

(Recommended between April and October)

O.K. I admit it—I am in love with San Francisco. I have spent a great deal of time in nearly every nook and cranny of Europe, circled the Pacific, been just about everywhere. But San Francisco remains my favorite area in the world in which to live. Why? Well, the pace is less hectic than in most major American metropolitan areas, yet there is an extraordinary variety of arts and entertainment, equal on a per capita basis to any great cultural center. The city's range of exciting dining places is a restaurant-goer's dream come true (for more on this dearest-to-my-heart subject, see "Why is San Francisco Such a Great Restaurant City?"). Its weather is politely moderate but should February's wetness get you down, you can always hop an hour's flight to Palm Springs to bask in the sun or drive only a few hours to the finest ski slopes in the West.

Perhaps most important is that San Francisco doesn't close you in. Its constant around-the-corner views, the consciousness of sky, the briskness of ocean breezes all alleviate the stifling asphalt-jungle aura of New York, or Tokyo, or Milan. And should you desire an even greater respite from steel and concrete, all you need do is drive but a few miles to find yourself in beautiful, unspoiled country, where pine needles crackle underfoot, the surf pounds and the stars are touchable. And this is exactly what we are going to share on our special side trip up the coast.

145

Almost all guidebooks to the San Francisco area list a visit to Carmel at the top of their "out-of-town" trips. And perhaps I would have done so, too—thirty years ago. But Carmel has changed. It has become the shopping mecca for thousands upon thousands of visitors who clog the narrow streets endlessly circling the town's few square blocks in search of that nonexistent parking place. So while I do recommend a visit to Carmel a few pages on, tying it in with a journey down the Big Sur Coast to the Hearst Castle, I believe the ideal change of pace from city life to the open spaces is achieved by heading north to Mendocino.

THE FIRST DAY

First we had better decide what to take along. Let's see. You will need only informal wear. The one restaurant which insists upon neckties, I boycott. So take some casual sunny weather togs (it never gets scorching hot, but it can be warm), as well as some more sturdy stuff just in case the fog is in. Our destination—the Little River Inn, Highway 1, Little River, (707) 937-5942—has a 9-hole golf course, while a few miles away in the midst of the giant redwoods is the Mendocino Tennis Club (for reservations: 707-937-0007). So throw in the appropriate sports gear. The area also claims some fine state parks with miles of hiking trails, so if you are into that—as I am—take along your hiking shoes. Should fishing be your hobby, steelhead and salmon abound here. Nightlife is absent from this rural scene so bring along your dominoes, cards and some good books . . . or just your desire for quiet.

Whenever I travel, I like to get started early. I like early morning departures, either train, plane, bus or car. It seems to me that if I plan to leave later in the day, I just fritter away the morning hours waiting to go and rechecking to see if I have packed everything. But today your departure time is dependent upon which route you elect to take.

In previous editions of this guide I have always recommended a leisurely non-freeway route (Highway 1) which takes about 5 hours to travel, not counting any lengthy stops. The reason for recommending it so highly is its awesome scenic beauty.

However, there are two drawbacks to this route. First of all, much of it is pretty rough driving—mile upon mile of hairpin turns on narrow roads carved out of mountainsides that fall off to the surf below. Secondly, I have never found anyplace memorable at which to lunch along the way. And thirdly, my favorite place in Mendocino closes at 2 p.m.; therefore, reaching it on time is chancy even with a fairly early departure.

Thus, in this edition I will suggest a second route. It is faster, and while not as totally spectacular it is quite beautiful. An even more important consideration is that it passes right by the front door of one of Northern California's most exciting restaurants—the New Boonville.

Knowing those facts, the decision is yours. If you decide on the longer, more scenic route, I suggest a hearty pre-departure breakfast; if you take the second easier route, have a light breakfast since in only two hours you will be at the New Boonville.

So, with the car packed, head out to now familiar Van Ness Avenue, turn left onto Lombard Street and cross the Golden Gate Bridge.

About 4 miles north of the bridge, you will see a sign indicating "Mill Valley, Stinson Beach, Highway 1." This is the dividing point of the two routes. If you have decided on the longer spectacular route, take this turnoff to the right; if you are taking the shorter way, via the New Boonville, stay on the freeway heading north.

Let me accompany those taking the longer, Highway 1 route for a few pages. Even if you are not going this way, you might want to find out what you are missing.

You will remember the first few miles of Highway 1, if you took the Muir Woods outing recommended on the Third Day's schedule. However, Highway 1 soon becomes filled with twists and turns as it roller-coasters over the foothills to the ocean. From the crests of some of the headlands on a clear day, you can see forever . . . and that includes portions of San Francisco even though you are now in the country. After dipping to sea level at Muir Beach, Highway 1 shoots abruptly upward again and suddenly below you are the sands of Stinson Beach.

The next stretch is along gentle cattle-grazing land and through sleepy little hamlets like Olema and Marshall, where the population figures on the road signs number less than the guest list at a successful city cocktail party. Along Tomales Bay you will see oyster farms, but unfortunately, these oysters are enormous and not particularly appealing, at least to me.

Highway 1 now cuts inland through more dairy land and through Bodega Bay. In this little town, known for its salmon fleet, Alfred Hitchcock shot his classic "The Birds." Remember when Tippi Hedren was suddenly attacked by that first gull? Well, it was right in the middle of that small harbor on your left. By the way, if you got away late and will not be able to reach Little River (still some 3 hours away) in time for the 2:00 p.m. lunch curfew, you might lunch here at The Tides. The only dish I have enjoyed here is the salmon, but then salmon is *the* fish along this entire route and you will be savoring it superbly prepared at the Little River Inn, so I do hope you love salmon!

Ten miles further at Jenner, Highway 1 crosses a high bridge spanning the mouth of the Russian River; and 13 miles later brings you in sight of Fort Ross. Not too long ago, Highway 1 ran right through this old wooden fort but in order to better preserve the historic spot, the highway now skirts the high stockade. If you wish to visit the fort, you must park in a lot to the left of Highway 1 and take a long walk. If you did not stop at Bodega Bay, this is a great place for a welcome leg-stretch.

Fort Ross was constructed in 1812, when a party of Russians accompanied by native Alaskans landed there. Their purpose in erecting the fort was multiple: to plant wheat for their Alaskan settlements, to hunt for otter, and to trade with the Spaniards who owned California but had advanced only as far north as San Francisco. In fact, the Spaniards never knew about Fort Ross until it was too late. And as you can see, the fort's strategic position enabled the Russians to decline all "invitations" to leave. Only a couple of buildings still stand and even they have been restored. In the northeast corner is a chapel, while in the southeast is an octagonal blockhouse with gun emplacements facing the sea, the primary access to the fort until the 1920's.

After leaving Fort Ross, continue on up Highway 1 for about 75 miles to the Little River Inn, our destination.

Now then, for those traveling up Highway 101, the route is almost arrow-straight, through Marin county's bedroom communities. After Santa Rosa, you travel through vast vineyards framed by rolling hills. Right past Cloverdale (about 78 miles from San Francisco) take a turnoff to the left marked "Highway 128 Boonville." And in about 27 miles you will find yourself in the small town of Boonville, which no one had heard of before the advent of the New Boonville, one of Northern California's finest new restaurants.

New Boonville, Highway 128, Boonville, (707) 895-3478, (open daily for lunch and dinner; reservations advised). The New Boonville's success is truly phenomenal. How could any restaurant so remote and far removed from San Francisco gain such popularity that on summer weekends it is difficult to obtain a table without reservations far in advance? The answer obviously is that their cuisine hits some kind of enormously responsive chord, appealing to a vast segment of today's restaurant-goers who want simplicity in concept, precision in execution and only the finest of strictly fresh ingredients. And the New Boonville fulfills each of these criteria as few other similarly styled restaurants do.

Unlike many restaurants of this genre, the New Boonville has a hard liquor license and its bar is stocked with a variety of unusual single-malt Scotch whiskeys. Served neat, a glass can make a decidedly keen appetite whetter. Inside the uncluttered—bordering on severe—dining areas there is almost a reverential quiet. Extremely knowledgeable serving persons explain the a la carte menu's offerings in hushed tones—acolytes at some sacred ritual.

The menu continually changes, depending on what is available. And that can mean what is pickable in their own garden out back! But here is the kind of thing you can expect: fresh egg noodles tossed with butter, walnuts and sage; the most succulent grilled chicken breast flavored with a translucent sauce based on a local Sauvignon blanc; a moistly tender grilled pork loin enhanced by a soy-ginger-cilantro marinade; red and green cabbage deftly braised with rosemary, etc. Each dish will be prepared from scratch and therefore your lunch will be leisurely. But I would wait an hour for the likes of their semolina pudding with preserved spring fruit. The wine list concentrates exclusively on vintners of the Anderson Valley, where Boonville is located. Try a Gewurztraminer from Navarro or if you like Zinfandels, treat your taste buds to an Edmeades Crapusci Vineyards bottling.

The Guide Michelin, that gastronomic Bible of France, awards its loftiest three stars to restaurants it deems "worthy of a special journey." The New Boonville is certainly right in that class. But how lucky for us that the road to Mendocino just happens to pass its front door. Oh yes, New Boonville accepts *no* credit cards and a 15% service charge is included. Worth every penny.

After perhaps a walk through the vegetable-herb garden in the back, you are ready to continue on your way to Little River. To do so, simply remain on Highway 128 as it crosses the lovely Anderson Valley. If you are not planning to return via this route, you might consider making a stop at some of the wineries along the way to sample and perhaps purchase. Many like Navarro are impossible to find in liquor stores.

On leaving the Anderson Valley, Highway 128 takes you through a breathtaking redwood forest and on to the Pacific Ocean, some 30 miles after Boonville. After intersecting with Highway 1, head north for only 8 more miles to the Little River Inn.

The Inn proper, a white Maine-style building dating from 1853, stands on a small rise to the right of the highway, looking out over an inlet and the endless Pacific. Where pioneers once stood watch for arriving sailing vessels which brought long-awaited news from the East and fresh provisions, you now can stand watch for a salmon fleet or perhaps even some migrating gray whales.

Not too long ago, the Mendocino Coast around Little River was strictly a haven for fishermen. All they wanted ashore were a decent bed, a well-stocked bar, and wholesome no-nonsense grub. Then this incredibly beautiful coastline was "discovered" by vacationers and soon, the small town of Mendocino (just about 3 miles further up Highway 1) began to court fancier food, artsy galleries, "shoppes" with cute names, and the inevitable fume-spewing tour buses. Throughout this change, the Little River Inn has stayed pretty much the same, adding a new wing and cottages.

Now then, if you came up the coast route, Highway 1, and have not had lunch, I hope for your sake it is not 2 o'clock yet. Because that is when the Cafe Beaujolais, my favorite luncheon spot in the area, closes.

So if it is nearing 2 o'clock, drive past the Inn for three miles, turn left at the "Business District" sign into the town of Mendocino. Then turn right off Main Street onto Howard for one block, then right onto Ukiah to number 961, and dash into the unassuming little house that is the Cafe Beaujolais, Mendocino, (707) 937-5614, (open daily for breakfast and lunch).

I honestly doubt whether a canned or frozen vegetable—God forbid, a preservative!—has ever found its way into this bastion of freshness and culinary honesty. Just catch your breath while you bask in the luxuriant natural sweetness of a truly fresh Tomato Bisque or Cream of Carrot Soup. Or delve into the Garden Salad featuring greens of a country, fresh-picked liveliness rarely encountered in the city. For a main course, Beaujolais' crepes are a specialty. And on sampling the one filled with both smoked and fresh salmon, blanketed in a creme fraiche sauce, you understand why immediately. For something deliciously offbeat, the Black Bean Chili is the ultimate vegetarian bean dish, enlivened with cumin, coriander, and cheese, but pacified by sour cream.

For dessert, Beaujolais usually whips up one of those diet-defying chocolate things, such as a ground nut-textured, sensuous Queen Mother's Torte.

By the way, if the Beaujolais serves superb lunches, it is even more famous for its breakfasts. And it would be criminal for you to miss the opportunity to relish dishes such as their waffle of buttermilk, cornmeal and oatmeal. You can have it served with real, honest-to-God maple syrup, not that liquid sugar, imitation stuff! Your orange juice will be squeezed to order. And the Moccalate, a delicious blending of chocolate and coffee, is my favorite breakfast beverage in all the world! So schedule a breakfast visit to Cafe Beaujolais sometime during your stay.

After a final sip of some of Beaujolais' peerless coffee, it is time to drive the three miles back to the Little River Inn and check in.

There is no need for me to plan the remainder of your afternoon. You will want to unpack and rest up after that long drive. If it is sunny, you might wish to walk down to the beach at Van Damme State Park adjacent to the inn. Otherwise, just collapse in front of your view of the ocean and relax.

For dinner, there are two places I can recommend—the Little River Inn and the tiny Little River Restaurant, directly across the highway and adjacent to the Post Office.

Little River Restaurant, Highway 1, Little River, (707) 937-4945 (dinner served Thursday through Sunday; reservations advised). Here is a pocket-sized little restaurant—seating about 18 people—that turns out very respectable dinners at comfortably modest prices. If you choose the soup of the day you may come up with a lovely melange of mushrooms and zucchini. The salad is one of those composites of several greens, beans, etc. that most people like but I find meaningless. The leg of lamb arrives buttery tender and surprisingly rare—hallelujah! The filet of beef is enrobed in a noble red-wine sauce. And all entrees are served with fresh and handsomely handled vegetables. A rich homemade walnut-chocolate tart is also a product of a kitchen so tiny the chef must move from the range when the refrigerator door is opened! A bargain, and just perfect for tonight.

THE SECOND DAY

Since these few days on the Mendocino Coast should be free of all pressures and big city regimens, you will not find me putting together an hour-by-hour activity schedule for you. Just do your own thing. But if you don't mind, I will join you for breakfast, a positively great meal at Little River Inn.

You can start with a brimming glass of freshly-squeezed orange juice. Yes, it's not "reconstituted from concentrate" or any of that ersatz orange stuff astronauts supposedly thrive on. This usually sets my palate up for a big plate of the inn's Swedish Hot cakes, piping hot and delectably light, accompanied by a few strips of crisp thick-cut bacon. Eggs are done any way you want them. There is plenty of toast, but I cannot resist the freshly baked muffins. Sometimes they are banana, sometimes blueberry, but always superb.

Anyhow, with the stick-to-your-ribs lumberjack breakfast under your belt, some type of exercise is called for. So how about heading to the golf course or tennis courts or going for a nice long hike? And with Van Damme Park right next door and Russian Gulch State Park just a few miles up Highway 1, you have a couple of great options.

Actually, you can begin your hike into Van Damme Park's Fern Canyon right from the Little River Inn, without even setting foot on the highway. For right from the Inn's driveway, there is a trail that takes you above Highway 1 and directly to the park's entrance. Here you turn right and head into the park. In minutes you are past the campers and tents and heading into a narrow, shady canyon, its walls covered with literally millions of ferns as well as towering redwoods and Douglas fir. And depending on the time of the year, you will also see a vast variety of blooming plants, including trillium, calypso orchids, and rhododendron.

The hike in through Fern Canyon is an easy one. However, if you wish to visit the Pygmy Forest, you will have to take a steeper trail up to the crest. And the Pygmy Forest should not be missed. Here just about every tree which grows in the area can be seen in miniature form. Due to a lack of nutrients in this particular patch of soil, fully matured firs and pines reach a height of only a few feet. It's an intriguing sight. (If you cannot make the trek on foot, you can reach the Pygmy Forest by car. Just take the Little River Airport Road, which hits Highway 1 just south of Little River, and drive about three and a half miles inland.)

There is another nearby park, Russian Gulch Park, which offers more fine hikes—one of a similar nature which ends at a lovely waterfall, another which takes you out onto the wind-swept headlands. In addition, Russian Gulch Park provides a picnic area with a dramatic view of the ocean and the entrance to the gulch.

If you decide to enjoy Russian Gulch Park, you might wish to pick up those picnic provisions at the Main Street Delicatessen in Mendocino—it's right on your way. All you need do is head north up Highway 1 from the Little River Inn. Along Highway 1, you will pass grazing fields and old, tumble-down barns seemingly in wait for Andrew Wyeth to come by and capture on canvas the last of their kind. In about three miles, turn left into the town of Mendocino, swinging right onto Main Street. On one side is a bluff overlooking Mendocino Bay, while on the other are shops and a hotel dating from 1878. But more about that later. Right now we need to find the Main Street Delicatessen at number 45040 and pick up some provisions. This might include a bottle of wine from one of the local wineries.

With our mission completed, head back out of Mendocino the way you entered. But at the intersection with Highway 1, turn left a few miles north to Russian Gulch (turnoff on left of Highway). Right after passing the park entrance, where you will pay a small day-use fee, continue on ahead. Immediately on the right, take note of a turnoff, which would take you to the picnic area. But for now proceed straight ahead and soon you will pass under the bridge that arches high over the canyon's mouth. Drive through the camp to the furthest parking area. As you approach, on the right you will spot a trail sign indicating "South Trail."

When you park, you can decide which hike you wish to take. If you proceed straight ahead from the parking area, you will find a trail very similar to that at Van Damme Park. This one also follows a stream deep into a huge, fern-covered canyon. The reward at the end of a short but somewhat steep climb is lovely, 36-foot high Russian Gulch Falls. Your other choice is to visit the spectacular Mendocino headlands. To reach them, walk back to that "South Trail" marker and take that trail. It will first lead you up the south side of the canyon, then under the Highway 1 bridge and out onto the headlands. Here you will find yourself on a wildflower-covered, wind-swept bluff with the foam-spewing, crashing waves of the Pacific pounding below you. It is an awesome spot. And if you look across the canyon to the headlands on the north side, you will be able to spot your luncheon picnic area. When you have had enough of the majesty of the ocean's might, simply retrace your route to your car, then drive back up the same road by which you arrived. Before you reach the park exit, turn left into the picnic area for lunch. Even the most mundane ham sandwich tastes delicious when consumed on this spot after a nice long hike!

After lunch, you might enjoy a walk out onto this headland, but watch out for the poison oak! Here you can see the Devil's Punch Bowl, a sea-cut tunnel 200 hundred feet in length which has collapsed at its inland end to produce a hole 100 feet in diameter and 60 feet deep. However, the waves pushing through the tunnel only create the "blow-hole" effect during heavy storms, which hopefully is not the weather condition today!

On you way back to the inn, you should revisit the quaint town of Mendocino, to which we gave such short shrift earlier this morning. Therefore, on leaving the Russian Gulch Park, take Highway 1 to the right. Enter Mendocino via the same route you took just a few hours ago.

Of course, you may wish to just wander around the town, peeking into some of the shops. Many have quite interesting handicrafts by local artists. But there are two stops you should not miss.

The first is the Mendocino Hotel at 45080 Main Street. Be sure to drop into this 100-year old establishment, superbly restored to its Victorian elegance. (There are tours of the entire hotel on Saturdays at 1 p.m.)

Another compulsory stop for me is in the next block. Here in the tiny Marilyn Douglas Mendocino Jams & Jellies shop you can purchase some of the finest preserves you have ever tasted. If you took any of the hikes, you surely must have noticed the vast quantities of berries which grow in this area. Well, Marilyn Douglas preserves them without the use of any extenders or preservatives. Her Wild Blackberry and her Boysenberry are incomparable! Often, there are a few flavors to taste, so you can verify my high estimation on the spot. She will also ship her products anywhere in the U.S.A.

When you have had enough walking about, all you need do is return to Highway 1 and turn south to the Little River Inn. Once back there, I am sure I need not convince you just how soothing it would be to laze out on a chair overlooking the bay, and take in the sea and the high sky filled with white clouds. At times, I have done just that and perhaps with the distraction of a good book, soon found myself light-years removed from San Francisco and routine.

After a day of hiking, golfing or tennis, if you are like

me you probably dread dressing up and driving off somewhere to dine. And that is just what you don't have to do! Because you can discover a delicious dinner right in the casual dining room of the Little River Inn.

Here you start off with a fine homemade soup. On Friday, it is one of the best Boston Clam Chowders this side of Beacon Hill. Milky white, chock-full of tender clams, with a judicious amount of potato and onion, it is happily free of gelatinous thickeners and other alien intruders. Next comes a pleasant salad.

For a main course, do not miss the salmon, if it is in season. With the salmon fleet in view off the front porch, you can be assured that it will be fresh. And the Little River's kitchen understands that the preservation of the salmon's sweet moistness is achieved by judicious cooking. Therefore, your order will be broiled—which is the way I ask it be prepared—just long enough to cook it through, but not to dehydrate it. For those who prefer meat, there is quite a respectable New York Steak.

One aspect of the inn's cooking that has changed, and for the better, is their vegetables. At one time, all you could hope for was canned corn. Now, I have encountered a smooth squash puree on one evening and Chinese-crisp green vegetables on another.

For dessert—just about the best Berry Cobbler around. Served piping hot (the whipped-cream topping transformed into creamy rivulets), it tantalizes your taste buds with an ideally slight undersweetness. A good soup, impeccable salmon, and down-home berry cobbler. What more could you ask for?

THE THIRD DAY

Actually, this day could just as easily be the fourth or the fifth day, depending upon how much time you want to spend in this wonderful area. But eventually, it will be time to start back to San Francisco. And if today is the day for your return, I have some suggestions.

As I explained on the way up, there are two basic routes you can take. One is to simply take Highway 1 all the way back to San Francisco. It certainly is the most scenic although tortuous. But if you have more than one driver in your party, you might do just that. However, if you wish to make better time, it is best to head inland and meet up with Highway 101. This can easily be done by driving about 7½ miles south on Highway 1, then onto Highway 128 for 56 miles to Highway 101 and then for about 80 mostly freeway miles to San Francisco. (This was the route north which I recommended to those who preferred to avoid the difficulties of Highway 1 and who wished to lunch at the sensational New Boonville. In fact, if you took Highway 1 up, you certainly should make this your return route and lunch at the New Boonville.)

Or . . . if you wish for a longer stay in this wonderful area of California, and if you have read ahead to make the necessary reservations, you could continue your Northern California tour by now heading to the Benbow Inn in Garberville, 445 Lake Benbow Drive, (707) 923-2124. Here in the midst of the mighty redwoods stands this National Historical Landmark, which has played host to international figures and localites alike since 1926. Recently restored, the Benbow welcomes you with graciousness, charm and such niceties as English tea with scones in the afternoon. During the day you can play tennis, take horseback rides, golf on the nine-hole course, swim in Benbow Lake or hike through the magnificent redwood forests. In the evening, a surprisingly fine restaurant welcomes you. The Benbow is a cherished getaway for scores of Bay Area residents, so reservations should be made as far in advance as possible.

To reach the Benbow, head north on Highway 1 through Fort Bragg. There at 356 North Main Street you may wish to make a quick pit stop at the Flying Bear, a candy shop that creates the definitive Rocky Road Candy. Equally spectacular are their Chocolate Truffles, Creamy Chocolate Mints, and Belmonts which are a combination of vanilla cream, dark chocolate and crunchy almonds. They are great for snacking in the car.

Continue on through Fort Bragg, remaining on Highway 1 through Westport and Rockport and on to Leggett. At Leggett you join up with Highway 101, taking it for approximately twenty-one miles to the Benbow Inn. (Total distance from the Little River Inn to the Benbow Inn is about 78 miles.) After your stay at the Benbow, you simply take Highway 101 right back to San Francisco.

Whether you went on to the Benbow or came directly back to San Francisco from the Little River Inn, you will need a dining recommendation for the night. I'll give you a couple, the first being totally unlike any of the cooking you experienced on your trip north.

Tommaso's, 1042 Kearny Street off Broadway (398-9696; open nightly except Monday; no reservations), is physically located within a tassle's throw of North Beach's honky-tonk topless row; however, its heart and soul lie near Naples. When you first open the heavy front door, you will be greeted by the strong aroma—perfume to me—of an oak fire. Over its glowing coals, Tommaso's bakes their pizzas. But stop! Do not make a mistake you always will regret by saying, "Oh, pizza. I don't want a pizzeria." Tommaso's is not a pizzeria; it just happens to be one of the finest Italian restaurants in town. Yet, because its origins are Neapolitan, it has proudly featured for over 50 years that area's specialty—pizza. And this is real pizza, not that cardboard stuff so readily available in drive-ins, dime stores and even movie theaters! Here, at Tommaso's, is the place for you to discover what pizza can and should be.

I usually begin my dinner with two or three salads. Why so many? Well, I never can decide whether I crave the fresh broccoli or the fantastic string beans, or the temptingly sweet roasted green peppers. So why be frustrated? I order a selection of them for the table and eat Chinese style! Then, I cannot resist an order of the Shrimp with Marinara Sauce. Then, and only then, am I ready for my pizza. I will leave your choice of topping up to you. But remember, a truly great pizza is not made of topping alone. Just take a look at the dough—it has a lovely full-bodied flavor all its own; its edges are light and fluffy. Now, that is pizza!

However, often I by-pass a pizza and opt for Tommaso's glorious Calzone. A calzone is made of the same ingredients as a pizza, but here the dough is not flat but rather folded over the mozzarella, ricotta, sausage, tomato sauce, and mushroom filling. It's an Italian turnover *par excellence!* If there are more than two in your party, I would certainly order one pizza and the Calzone #14.

Of course, you can select one of the many other dishes as your main course, although I avoid their veal creations. And a word of caution: When ordering a pasta, inquire if the kitchen has time to cook yours to order, al dente. Tommaso's can become extremely crowded and the pastas, at times, reveal the kitchen's haste by being pre-cooked and even overly so. Soft pasta is a cardinal sin in Italy that can condemn the chef to Dante's lowest level in that big pizza oven down below. So do as the Italians do and make sure your pasta is done right.

For dessert, inquire if the canoli have been refrigerated for long. (By the way, the friendly family at Tommaso's never seems to mind such probing.) If the canoli is fresh, these crispy tubes stuffed with sweetened ricotta are sensational. However, if they have served time in the refrigerator, they can become soggy, losing their most endearing quality. The coffee is suavely Neapolitan and an ideal way to end your evening's visit to bella Napoli. Not to be missed! (If you are driving directly to Tommaso's from the redwood country, simply take Lombard Street from the Golden Gate Bridge; turn right on Van Ness; then left down Broadway to Kearny Street.)

My alternate offering is best suited for those who are not lunching at New Boonville, but would like to experience something like it in San Francisco. And that is what you can do at the Post Street Bar & Cafe, 632 Post Street (928-2080; open for dinner Tuesday through Saturday; for lunch Monday through Friday; reservations advised).

I first was attracted to the Post Street Bar & Cafe because it offers theatre goers attending either the Curran,

Geary or Marine's Memorial Theaters a great place to dine within walking distance. However, once I was lured there by that attraction, I was soon won over by its innovative style of cooking and its pleasant, unfussy service.

You will note that the Post Street is a Bar and Cafe, not Bar and Grill. Therefore, you will not find a host of grilled fish and meats, as you would, for example, at the superb Hayes Street Grill. Here the menu is limited to about six main courses, a daily seafood special and a daily pasta special. But even with so short a menu, you will not be bored.

For example, their Caesar Salad is not the heavy, overly tossed mess it often is. Rather the delicately tender hearts of Romaine are treated to top-grade olive oil and imported Parmesan cheese, and spinkled with home-made garlicky croutons. The special pasta is always unusual, such as a very spicy linguini with smoked pork, red and green peppers, artichoke hearts, all moistened with a red pepper butter. The daily seafood special might be something like grilled prawns, with roe intact, treated to an avocado salsa and served with magnificent melange of black-eyed peas and black beans!

As I have said before, I am partial to rib-eye steaks, and Post Street does a fine job with theirs. Their Roast Leg of Lamb is also a winner, and I risk being served what at times can be a slightly overcooked Medallions of Home-Cured Pork Loin just to savor their marvelous hash-brown sweet potatoes. Vegetables are always absolutely fresh.

With desserts, made daily on the premises, Post Street can do no wrong. Their Lemon Meringue Pie is wonderfully tart not Jello sweet. While their Apple-Rhubarb Crisp can make macho men weep. Or the Gingerbread with bourbon-touched whipped cream, dusted with nutmeg. Inventive cuisine combined with distinctive touches of down-home, handsomely served in a fireplace-warm atmosphere makes Post Street Bar & Cafe a find! Upper moderate price range.

A Trip to Yosemite National Park

"Yosemite? Oh, I haven't been there in years. I understand it's completely ruined," might be a reaction you encounter if you tell a San Franciscan you are planning a trip there. For years, newspaper accounts of vast overcrowding and of camper caravans belching so much exhaust that the smog blots out the view, have contributed to the popular belief that Yosemite is finished. Well, as once happened to Mark Twain, the reports of Yosemite's death have been greatly exaggerated. Today, El Capitan's "glacier-sculpted face of granite" still looms above the valley floor; sunbeams still "play with spray and mist in rainbow colors" at the base of thundering waterfalls; and when winter's chill leaves the land, the brooks still "sing carols and glees to the spring." Yes, you can still experience these wonders of Yosemite, just as John Muir—the man who wrote the above eloquent words—did many, many years ago.

Mother Nature has not changed but, like everything else, Yosemite has. Today, there are a great many more people in our nation than there were twenty or fifty years ago. And today, there is more leisure time than ever before. So with this greater opportunity for relaxation, more and more people have begun to explore what conservationists and naturalists like John Muir have been writing about for years—the experience of the natural beauties of our world. Therefore, America's system of national parks (one of the greatest assets this country can proudly claim) has become *the* vacationland. And Yosemite is high on the list. In fact, because of its easy access to major metropolitan areas, it has to bear more than its burden of increased interest. Consequently, especially in the peak summer season, there is no doubt that crowds jam the park to bursting. However, the incredible grandeur and drama of Yosemite cannot be eradicated so easily.

My two favorite times of year to visit the park are spring and fall. In the spring, the valley is at its most spectacular, for the waterfalls, fed by the melting snow, are at their fullest and their thunder is an awesome proclamation of the beginning of a new cycle of life. In the fall, the valley is garbed in a more serene air, the leaves are turning, and the squirrels and chipmunks become more brazen as they busily hunt for their winter stores. Although winter snows can indeed transform Yosemite into a dazzling white wonderland, storms can also curtail my favorite pastime, hiking; while in the summer, the crowds fence me in.

If you must visit Yosemite in peak season, you can get away from much of the hubbub by taking hikes away from the more populated areas. And believe me, Yosemite's back paths will open up for you a mountain paradise. If you do not want to backpack all the way in, you still will be amazed at how just a quarter-mile further along a secluded trail leads into the quiet beauty of nature. More than likely, you will still meet a few folks along the way, but their friendly, "we are all one," murmured greetings blend with the environment.

In order to enjoy these hikes, you must come prepared. For the lesser hikes, that means with what the British would call "sensible shoes." For more arduous climbs, proper hiking boots and equipment are necessary. Also, if you would like to try your hand (and feet) at more strenuous mountaineering or rock climbing, there is a school located in the valley.

Yosemite's lakes and rivers offer invigorating swimming opportunities, although you might find the warmer waters of the pools at Yosemite Lodge and/or the Ahwahnee Hotel a little more congenial. Seeing the valley by bicycle or horseback is possible; fishing licenses and tackle are available in the village store. For more citified sporting, the Ahwahnee has two tennis courts and a putting green; and the Wawona Hotel, an hour's drive from the valley, has a 9-hole course. So after reading this list of possible Yosemite activities, be sure you take with you the appropriate gear. Oh, yes, that reminds me: men should be sure to include in their suitcases a tie and jacket, requirements for admission into the Ahwahnee dining room at night.

As with most national parks, one concessionaire handles all the accommodations. In this case, it is the Yosemite Park and Curry Company. In the valley proper, lodgings are provided to fit any budget. The most economical and understandably Spartan are the canvas tent-cabins at Camp Curry—with the rooms and cabins at Yosemite Lodge slightly more costly. The "deluxe" way of life is evident at the glorious Ahwahnee Hotel, one of my favorite hotels in the U.S. For reservations at any of these locations, call (209) 252-4848 or write to Yosemite Park and Curry Company Reservations, 5410 E. Home, Fresno, CA 95727. And make your reservations as far in advance as possible. Yosemite hotels are booked at least one month in advance during the peak season, and almost that far ahead for the rest of the year. I have always found reservations to be handled efficiently, with a written confirmation.

Thousands of campsites and trailer sites are available in the valley. Reservations for them can easily be made through Ticketron (392-SHOW; small service fee; outlet located in Emporium on Market Street between Fourth and Fifth Streets). If you wish to camp out, reserving ahead is the best way to insure a site.

Although I have never pitched a tent in Yosemite in all the years I have been regularly visiting the park, I have upgraded myself from a Camp Curry tent to a balconied room at the Ahwahnee. And to be quite candid, it didn't take me long to accomplish this because I fell in love with the Ahwahnee at first sight. It really does not look like a hotel but rather reminds me of some enormous stone and wood hunting lodge built at the base of granite cliffs which arch hundreds of feet above it. And the interior is a haven for those of us who suffer claustrophobia in the cramped lobbies of most of today's hotels. The two-storied lounge has two fireplaces each as spacious as some hotel rooms! And wait until you see the dining room with its vaulted ceiling and enormous windows looking out onto a meadow.

With all this breathing room, the Ahwahnee seems almost impervious to the crowded conditions in the village. Even when the hotel is completely filled, as it invariably is, there is enough quiet space for everyone. Well, more about the Ahwahnee when you arrive in Yosemite. Now, it's time you get going.

THE FIRST DAY

I have devoted as much thought to your departure time for Yosemite as I have to the route you should travel. And you will understand why as you read on. As I have mentioned before, I am of the "early departure" school of travel. However, Yosemite presents a problem. Although the Ahwahnee now posts a check-out time of 11:00 a.m. (certainly an inhospitable change from their more leisurely 2:00 p.m. of years ago!), they caution that rooms may not be ready for occupancy until 3:00 p.m. And an even more discouraging sign is posted at the Yosemite Lodge, upping their check-in hour to an unbelievable 6:00 p.m.! Therefore, if you arrive at either the hotel or lodge early in the day, you can find yourself tired from a long drive with nowhere to go except to a lobby chair, to wait and wait.

Also, while San Francisco has long been a restaurant-goer's mecca, once outside its furthest boundary, you find yourself in a gastronomic desert with Denny's and Howard Johnson's as relay posts. So I recommend you enjoy a considerable brunch in the city at Sears', 439 Powell Street, between Post and Sutter (986-1160), and then set off for Yosemite at . . .

10:30 a.m. Have the desk clerk in your hotel direct you to the nearest on-ramp to the San Francisco-Oakland Bay Bridge. When you have crossed to the East Bay side, follow the signs to Interstate 580, a truck-prohibited stretch which enables you to skirt Oakland. Soon, 580 swings eastward, crossing a range of coastal hills and on into the upper reaches of the mighty San Joaquin Valley. It won't be long before you will see a sign indicating "580 to Interstate 5, Fresno, Los Angeles"; take this swing to the right.

As any map will show you in full detail, Yosemite is accessible via three basic routes from the San Francisco area. The seemingly straightest, as-the-crow-flies trek would be the northern course, via Highway 120. Although this route appears to be the shortest, the last stretch is a tortuous, long, narrow mountain road with few turnouts for slow-moving cars. Also, this approach is closed in the winter.

The California Automobile Association recommends the middle route, which would have you leave Interstate 580, taking Highway 132 to Highway 99, then south to Merced where you join Highway 140 through Mariposa to Yosemite Valley. This route is regarded as the quickest (approximately 4½ hours) and it is the one by which you will return to San Francisco after your stay. My perennial path to Yosemite takes about 5 hours, but I consider the additional half-hour of driving a wise investment that will pay off in a grand visual dividend at the end of the drive.

You see, Yosemite Valley is cut lengthwise by the Merced River. Arriving by the two northern routes, you enter the valley by a road which follows the river's north bank, which gives you a gradual awareness of the mammoth cliffs and domes that wall the valley. The southern route, however, passes through the long Wawona tunnel on the more elevated south bank of the river. And on exiting the tunnel, the entire panorama of the valley is suddenly thrust upon you, as though you had just pushed open the doors of a vast cathedral with granite pillars rising thousands of feet above the floor. After having experienced this view dozens of times, I still break into goose bumps whenever I emerge from the Wawona tunnel into Yosemite's valley.

So, if you wish to share this memorable moment, you must continue down Interstate 580, ignoring the "Yosemite, Highway 132" sign, to Interstate 5, California's most super of super-highways. Stretching before you will be a seemingly endless ribbon of concrete, running arrowstraight as far as the eye can see. On your right is the Diablo Mountain Range—not the colossal granite giants you will see keeping watch over Yosemite but rather grass-covered, softly molded hills, often cultivated with fruit trees and vegetable crops. On the left, you will catch a view of the gigantic California aqueduct, a 500-mile engineering miracle which carries the run-off from Northern California's mountains to the Los Angeles area. And off in the distance lies the fertile San Joaquin Valley.

Soon, another Yosemite sign will tempt you to Highway 140 but ignore this one, too. The exit you want is Highway 152 East, marked "Los Banos" which, for 42 miles, takes you across the heart of the valley, passing miles of cotton fields, one of California's biggest crops. Highway 152 then merges with southbound Highway 99; 10 miles later, you will exit from 99 to the right, at the sign indicating "Millerton Lake, Yosemite."

Immediately after taking this exit, turn left onto the overpass which carries you to the east side of the freeway. Continue on ahead, crossing the railroad tracks and swinging onto Cleveland Avenue. Proceed along Cleveland for about 1½ miles, then swing right over a small bridge. Immediately after the bridge, turn left onto Highway 145; here, there is a sign indicating the direction to Yosemite. Fourteen miles later, turn left onto Highway 41, now heading north through the Sierra Nevada foothills to the park. Within a few miles, you will notice that the figures on the elevation markers increase as you climb to 5,120 feet to the park's entrance.

2:45 p.m.   At the entrance, you will be required to pay an auto permit fee. Be certain to save the receipt since you may be called upon to surrender it when leaving the park. The ranger stationed at the entrance also will hand you a copy of *Yosemite Guide*, a biweekly publication containing a wealth of information about the park and what events may be taking place during your stay. If you do not receive a copy, ask where you may pick one up.

Once in the park, you must make a decision. If you are weary, you will probably want to turn left and proceed straight to your destination, the Ahwahnee Hotel, still 45 minutes away. However, if you have been sharing the driving duties or are not that tired, you may wish to turn right for 2 miles to the Mariposa Grove where the "Big Trees," the redwoods, reach up into the heavens. Not too many years ago, you were allowed to drive right into the grove. Now, with the vast influx of visitors, a parking area has been constructed from which you can take a free tram ride through the entire grove. From the tram's open carts, you will be able to feel the awesome strength of these redwoods, the largest plants known to man.

Even native Californians, accustomed to seeing these giant redwoods, never fail to be somewhat amazed by them. But the impression they make on first-time viewers is often something to write about . . . just as this beautiful encounter was set into words in the *Yosemite Guide:*

"It was the last stop of the tour of the Mariposa Grove of Giant Sequoias. The evening light was already creating rays of shadows. A small, ancient man ignored the reasonings of his family and left the tram. He carefully selected a spot to sit, and walked slowly and purposely to it. There he viewed the massive, ancient tree for the first time alone. As his family left, his grandson ran down to join the man. Later they would both board the next tram back down to the parking area. But for now, the man studied the tree and thought. Finally, he bowed deeply and got up. 'He has traveled all the way from Japan,' the grandson explained to the ranger now shaking hands with the old man. 'He thanks you for it . . . for taking care of it.' The ranger didn't know Japanese, but obviously was understanding the man quite well."

This little vignette has two messages for me. First, these giant redwoods do require a reverent approach by man in order to absorb into his consciousness what the trees have been, what they are now, and what they will continue to be long after we are gone. And the other message is that they are still here not only because our government comprehends the need of conserving them, but also because there are marvelously devoted men and women— America's park rangers—who take care of them for us.

If you have taken this tram ride to the "Big Trees," it should now be about 4:00 p.m., time to head for the hotel. Simply drive back to the entrance gate and then proceed on toward Yosemite Village.

As you travel along this lovely road in the park, be careful to keep alert for deer and other animals, especially at this time of day when dusk is near. In the park, you will come across many animals, the most common being chipmunks, squirrels, deer and sometimes bear. Contact with all animals should be avoided for both your sake and theirs. First of all, you should not feed any of the animals. Naturalists tell us that while it may seem a kindness to offer food to a foraging fawn or cute little bushy-tailed squirrel, it is bad for them. This kind of pampering results in the animals losing their ability to forage for themselves; and when there are not enough visitors around, those animals spoiled in this fashion may die.

On the other side of the coin, any wild animal can be hazardous to your health. Bears are by far the most dangerous; however, even docile appearing deer have extremely sharp hoofs and smaller animals, such as chipmunks, can be rabid or carry parasites harmful to man. So just watch the animals, and please do it from a distance.

(A note: Along the road, you will spot a sign indicating that you may turn to a certain frequency on your radio in order to receive messages from the park rangers. Do so; it can be very informative.)

Continuing your drive to the Ahwahnee Hotel, you

will catch your first glimpse of the valley as you round a curve—but, in a matter of seconds, you are plunged into the darkness of the Wawona Tunnel. You are asked to turn on your lights because this is not a fancy tiled city tunnel but rather just a rough, dark passage blasted through the solid granite face.

Proceed through the tunnel slowly in order to pull into the parking area *immediately* on the left as you exit. And right there is your reward for taking the route I suggested—one of the greatest panoramas on our planet. And at this time of day, the sun is behind you, illuminating the whole spectacle in soft light, ideal for photography. If you are making this visit in the spring, your view will be further enhanced by the lovely Bridalveil Falls, a long slender ribbon of water which, when blown by the wind, billows out across the cliff's face like a sheer veil. Bridalveil Falls will be on the near right. For those interested in identifying the other major domes, falls and rocks, there is an outline map to assist you.

4:00-5:00 p.m.—depending on whether or not you went to Mariposa Grove and how much time you spent there. Although the changing light of the valley view has a mesmerizing effect, it is time to drive on to the hotel. Two urbanizing aspects which have now become part of the park are the use of one-way roads and a wealth of direction signs. With their help, you will have no difficulty locating the Ahwahnee Hotel at the far end of the valley, beyond the Village.

Upon your arrival at the hotel, an attendant will see that your luggage is delivered to the front desk while you are registering. He also will park your car, indicating its position on a small map printed on the envelope into which he will place your car keys.

As soon as you get to your room, call the dining room to make dinner reservations. Since the dining room serves non-guests as well, you must request the hour you wish as soon as possible or you may find it booked. After this is done, postpone those unpacking chores until after you've had tea in the Great Lounge. This late afternoon custom is a delightful holdover from a more relaxed and gracious era. And it suits the Ahwahnee ideally. Many is the time I have been out hiking for hours only to quicken my pace back to the hotel, knowing that a steaming cup of beautifully brewed tea was awaiting me. And after a long drive, you might find the tea just as rejuvenating before unpacking and dressing for dinner (remember: jacket and tie for gentlemen).

8:00 p.m. Unfortunately, the most exciting aspect of your meals at the Ahwanhee will be the splendor of the dining room. At night, the room takes on the aura of a candle-lit medieval banquet hall. At breakfast it is equally impressive with the light streaming in from tall windows which look out over the meadow. Would that the food were one-tenth as inspired!

Years ago, I was able to report that the Ahwahnee kitchen was "far above average for a hotel." Then it slid to "barely average." With a recent advertising campaign emphasizing visits of famed chefs during certain winter weekends, I thought the general level of cuisine might have been raised. But unfortunately, I found no improvement.

The language of the dinner menu certainly has taken a turn to the French with "coulis," "pommery mustard sauce" and "mousseline" bandied about. But what emerges from the kitchen bears little resemblance to French cuisine or even good ole American cookin'.

The adjective that best sums up the kitchen is "vapid." Almost without exception flavors were dulled, without focus. The shrimp in the cocktail supreme were water-logged and iodous. The house salad was what you would expect from a Denny's. The grilled breast of chicken possessed no discernible flavor of its own and its tomato coulis was acidic. The "milk fed" veal appeared to me to be closer in age to baby beef, pounded into senselessness. One could not even find safe haven in simpler fare, such as a huge listless slab of roast beef. Vegetables were all undeniably fresh, but steam-table sad. And I have not seen such huge, crude carrots since a winter in Moscow!

For desserts, the bittersweet chocolate mousse caused a friend to quip, "I didn't know Cool Whip came in beige." The Ahwahnee's pastry department, once the crowning glory of the kitchen, now presents pies which barely hold their own with Mrs. Smith's. The wine list, on the other hand, has been immeasurably improved and boasts some entries from California's finest vintners. But what a waste to offer these exciting bottles as accompaniment to such dull cuisine.

It really is a shame that the Ahwahnee's food continues to be so disappointing, because everything else is very pleasurable. A majority of the staff are young employees who appear to have been trained extremely well. And when they do make an occasional faux pas, they are so polite and good-natured that it seems insignificant. Would that the kitchen display such an open, honest style!

10:00 p.m.   After-dinner coffee, nowhere as expertly prepared as the afternoon tea, is usually available in the Great Lounge. And on some nights, there is dancing in the rather mundane Indian Room to the left of the entrance.

THE SECOND DAY

8:00 a.m.   Surely, you will not wish to sleep much later than this on your first morning in Yosemite. Awaiting you outside your hotel door is one of the world's most beautiful sights. And you do not even have to travel beyond the back lawn of the Ahwahnee to sense that special spirit which is Yosemite.

You know, I'll never forget the time I was sitting in the Great Lounge and upon glancing through the French doors, saw a lone nun peacefully sitting at one of the tables on the terrace. The sun, reflecting off the starched white wimple of her habit, radiated a halo effect in the morning light. She was holding her rosary beads, perhaps lost in prayer or simply deep in thought. I had to hold back an impulsive urge to walk over and ask if she thought Heaven would be more beautiful than this . . . for early morning in Yosemite is, indeed, heavenly.

After your stroll around the grounds, you probably will be ready for a more temporal consideration—breakfast. But first stop by the front desk to see if they have any trail maps on hand, and bring along your copy of the *Yosemite Guide.* Breakfast time will double as planning time.

In the morning, the cavernous Ahwahnee dining room completely sheds its mysterious, magical air of evening and dons a freshly scrubbed face, lit by the radiant morning light streaming through the wall of windows. After you have had your first cup of coffee, you can start perusing the maps and guide to decide what you would like to do today. Let me help.

A great deal of what you do and when you do it depends on: the length of your stay in Yosemite, your hiking ability, and the weather. Let's rule out the latter and assume the day is bright and sunny with only the usual few scattered Sierra clouds. The next consideration is just how much you like to hike or walk. In the valley, there are all kinds of walks—some with no inclines to tax your wind, others requiring fairly good stamina. Then, too, you should consider the length of your stay. As with sightseeing anywhere, be it in a complex of urban museums or in this cathedral of natural wonders, you simply cannot experience everything at once. Pacing your activities is essential for full enjoyment of them. With this in mind, I will recommend three walks.

One walk is to Mirror Lake. The entire walk is along a level paved road (or parallel path) without traffic. It is a little more than a mile in each direction, although you can make the return by shuttle bus. Mirror Lake is aptly named since Mt. Watkins is reflected in its still waters in a perfect double image.

And here, I would like to say a few words about the shuttle buses in use at Yosemite. Don't be turned off by them. Frankly, they are ideal for Yosemite and probably have contributed greatly in preserving the beauty of the park. You see, a few years ago, traffic in the park was becoming impossible with cars and campers turning every narrow road into a huge traffic jam. The park authorities faced with this problem wisely decided that instead of widening the roads and building more parking lots, thereby destroying huge areas of natural forests and meadows, they would offer visitors an easier means of access—shuttle buses. To encourage the use of these shuttles, many of the existing roads were torn up or narrowed, and then restricted to "shuttles only." The shuttle service goes just about everywhere in the valley, with the village as the main transfer point. And it is all free of charge!

A second walk (which is a bit more arduous) is a path to the base of Yosemite Falls. To take this walk, exit through the main automobile gate of the hotel. Soon, on the right, you will see a trail marker indicating that Yosemite Falls is a little over a mile away. The trail quickly climbs a bit as it skirts the small hospital and then the village. From this higher vantage point, there are some lovely views of the valley frequently filled with morning mist. Not so lovely, though, are the oft-appearing smog and campfire smoke which dull the view. However, it is an extremely pleasant walk and the reward at the end is Yosemite Falls, one of the most famous falls in the world. From here, you can take a shuttle back to the hotel.

My favorite hike (not walk) is to Vernal Falls. Take the shuttle from the Ahwahnee to the village and then transfer to a shuttle to Happy Isles, the starting point of the hike. Here, the wide and semi-paved trail starts upward, tracing the course of the Merced River on your right. As you hike higher, the sounds of the river cascading over the huge boulders become louder and louder. You will come to a bridge and from here, you will see Vernal Falls about three-quarters of a mile further up river. This is a good resting spot to consider whether you wish to go further or return to the valley floor.

If you do not want to hike much further, I do urge you to at least take the next quarter-mile hike to a lookout of Vernal Falls, clearly marked. Here, from the flat surface of an enormous granite boulder, you seem to be far closer to the falls than the very short distance you covered. It is a dream spot for photographs of those rainbows the sunbeams create in the falls' spray.

If you are ready and able for a further climb, I recommend you veer off this trail to the right at the sign marked "Nevada Falls." The sign indicates a distance of 2.4 miles, but I usually follow the trail only about 1.9 miles to a footpath marked "Yosemite Valley via Misty Trail," which leads back to the valley eventually. This higher climb reveals a fabulous look at Nevada Falls over which the Merced River plunges before coursing to Vernal Falls. And the footpath actually crosses right over the top of Vernal Falls from where you can watch the river close-up as it leaps over the sheer edge. Misty Trail then becomes a down staircase of sorts, cut into the rock face. If the falls are at their height, you will soon understand the significance of the name, Misty Trail.

Of course, you can go further afield either by car or bus transportation. For example, the bus will take you around the Mariposa Grove (if you failed to stop there on the way in) and to Glacier Point. Glacier Point is the 7,214-foot summit you see directly across the Ahwahnee grounds. It surely must be the spot where Whoever created Yosemite sat in satisfaction at His handiwork. You can also climb there by a rather steep 4-mile trail. But whether it is on wheels, horseback, or foot, the view from Glacier Point should be experienced.

Now, it is time you started. Remember to dress appropriately and wear the right kind of shoes. Also, if you will be gone for some time, the hotel has box lunches available which usually must be ordered the night before.

And speaking of lunch, if you do not return to the hotel, you might wish to lunch at Degnan's in the village—decent hamburgers, excellent French fries and salads. Also, in the same building housing Degnan's, there is a well-stocked delicatessen which you may wish to raid for picnic provisions. In any case, have a good day.

4:00 p.m.   By now you have probably returned to the

hotel, your feet and legs aching with the strain of the walks, but your eyes and soul filled with sights which will remain in your memory for years to come. A dip in the Ahwahnee pool might be nice—then tea, of course.

8:00 p.m.   Years ago, I used to look forward to donning jacket and tie after being in boots and hiking shorts all day, and walking into the Ahwahnee's beautiful dining room which seemed to be filled with a grand and festive air. But that was when the cuisine at least approached the elegance of dress. Now, I find I am often annoyed that I have to dress while the kitchen can "rough it." Therefore, when I am especially irked at this sham, I often retreat to Degnan's for dinner. It's not that the food is generally much better here; it's just that in the Loft's extremely informal atmosphere, "average" cooking is easier to tolerate.

YOUR THIRD OR FOURTH DAY

Yosemite would take months to fully experience. You would have to, for example, wait for the snows of winter to witness an entirely different but still poetic Yosemite. So now I will leave you on your own . . . perhaps to discover on a moonlit night, while walking through the meadow adjacent to the hotel, the sheer face of Half Dome bathed in a luminiscent blue, the likes of which you may never see again . . . or perhaps to learn about the whole world of bird life at home in Yosemite from a knowledgeable ranger on a 7:00 a.m. nature walk . . . or maybe to realize that a chair on the terrace looking up at the grey ancient face of Glacier Point is what relaxation is all about.

However, since I have delivered you to this Eden, I will help you find your way back to San Francisco. When you are ready to go (or find you must go), follow the signs indicating "Exits": Highway 140 is the one you will want. From the valley, it will take you out the El Portal Entrance through the town of Mariposa, and down to the table-top flatness of the San Joaquin Valley, passing enormous turkey farms and peach orchards. At Merced, pick up Highway 99 North, turning off 99 some 37 miles later onto Highway 132 West, which connects up with 580, which will take you right to the Bay Bridge.

Or . . . you might like to stop in Oakland for dinner at my favorite Mexican restaurant in the Bay Area.

La Mexicana, 3930 East 14th Avenue, Oakland (436-8388; open for lunch and dinner Wednesday through Sunday) looks like any unassuming storefront Mexican eatery, right down to the TV set in the kitchen area and the picture of President and Mrs. Kennedy along with one of the Virgin Mary. But there the resemblance to its competitors ends. The reason: it treats Mexican cuisine with pride and respect. Frankly, after dining in countless Bay Area Mexican restaurants, if I were blindfolded I could not tell one from the other by sampling their cooking. All seem to present the same vast combination plates, laden with leaden tacos, cardboard-textured enchiladas, et. al, awash in a non-descript sauce, wilting the seemingly requisite sprinkling of salad greens.

But at La Mexicana, for example, the Chile Rellenos are constructed from fresh chilis, gutted of their seeds and filled with cheese, then sauteed to a souffle-like lightness, and served with a tomato sauce than would be respected in any fashionable French kitchen. All the tortillas are made by hand—yes, all of them, not just a few for show. And they make special any dish in which they are employed—from the super chips with the excellent coarse guacamole to the delicious Enchilada al Horno, a baked enchilada. By the way, just taste the shredded filling in the chicken version of this dish. You can savor the care and finesse that went into cooking that bird! And for a truly fine taco, just try their version with chorizo! Oh yes, I would order all dishes as "side dishes", a couple per person, thus avoiding the filling rice and beans and enabling you to concentrate on the specialties. And for dessert, do not miss a slice of their Flan, not the usual vapid egg custard, but a rich quasi-cheesecake affair that makes all others pale in comparison. Plenty of Mexican beer to wash it all down with. No strolling guitars or flirtatious waitresses overflowing their low-cut peasant blouses. But an immaculate, unpretentious dining room and a smiling family that runs the show—which is the best culinary Mexican festival I know of in the Bay Area.

If honest, flavorful Mexican cooking of this high calibre appeals to you, especially after after the fractured-French of the Ahwanhee, you can easily reach La Mexicana by taking the "MacArthur Blvd—High Street" exit off Highway 580. Follow signs to High Street, which is the first light. Turn left on High and proceed to East 14th. A right on East 14th for two blocks and you are at La Mexicana. On leaving La Mexicana, you can continue your journey back to San Francisco very easily by reversing your direction on East 14th to 42nd Avenue. There make a right and you are on the approach to Highway 17. Follow the sign that indicates "Downtown Oakland" and once on Highway 17, you will soon see signs to San Francisco via the Bay Bridge.

After passing through the Treasure Island Tunnel with the San Francisco skyline now directly ahead, I often think of which view I love the more—the skyline of my home city, one of the most beautiful in the world, or Yosemite from the Wawona Tunnel. And I always end up saying, as you may now feel: "Each is unique. Each I love equally."

However, if you did not opt for La Mexicana, esthetics aside, you will probably have dinner on your mind. And what a pleasant prospect to be entering one of the country's best dining-out cities where a culinary palette of dazzling flavors awaits you. And since we have a car, we can easily drive out to the "Avenues" where we can delight in something a little exotic, like the elegant cooking of Vietnam.

Garden House, 133 Clement Street near Third Avenue (221-3655; open every night for dinner; lunch served only Friday through Sunday). Prior to the Vietnam War, I cannot recall a single Southeast Asian restaurant in San Francisco. But in the late '60s, Vietnamese and Thai restaurants began to open at an incredible rate and recently Cambodian restaurants are also cropping up.

Vietnamese cooking is often misallied with Chinese, a confusion Vietnamese chefs hasten to correct. They point out that their creations are "simpler," with fewer melanges of ingredients, and less oily. Also, in Vietnamese cuisine you will find mint and curry often used as seasonings, and raw bean sprouts employed for texture interest. In fact, the only real similarity between the two cuisines is the use of chopsticks.

If you are familiar with Vietnamese cuisine, you will no doubt recognize many of its great classics on the Garden House menu. For example, their Imperial Rolls are among the very best in town. These rolls filled with pork, shrimp and crab are deep fried and served with cold vermicelli-thin noodles, mint leaves, coriander and a dipping sauce. You place a little of each of the condiments along with a piece of the fried roll into a piece of lettuce leaf, wrap it all up and dip it into the sauce. Delicious. And since I have always found Vietnamese appetizers to be the most exciting aspect of their cuisine, do not hesitate in ordering several, such as their Barbecued Beef in Chao Fun. Into a thickish, gelatinous noodle (chao fun) is placed slightly spicy pieces of somewhat crispy barbecued beef and lettuce. I know it may sound a little strange, but what a wonderful study in flavor and texture contrasts. But perhaps my very favorite dish at Garden House is their remarkable Raw Beef Salad in which the paper-thin slices of beef have been tossed in a chili-peanut flavored dressing.

For main courses, the Chicken with Lemon Grass presents tender slices of chicken treated to a chili hot sauce, into which perhaps some coconut milk has been added. Garden House appears infallible when it comes to handling seafood, so be sure to try their Broiled Shrimp served on a bed of those vermicelli noodles or their Crispy Prawns, sauteed with a melange of barely cooked vegetables—cauliflower, snow peas, lettuce, onions, greenpeppers. My beverage at Garden House is 33 Beer.

That's not the quantity I consume, but the name of a French beer popular in Vietnam. And even if you drink several of them—which you can be tempted to do, given the spiciness of some of the dishes—the check will still be well within the moderate range.

A Four-Day Trip to Carmel,

Monterey, Big Sur and San Simeon

Almost every visitor to San Francisco has heard about Carmel and wants to see it. I think some knowledge about Carmel-by-the-Sea is important, however, before you decide to include this side trip in your stay.

If the person who told you about Carmel visited there twenty or thirty years ago, his or her experience would be somewhat different today. Carmel initially achieved its fame by being the epitome of the sleepy seaside hamlet, replete with a rather quaint artsy-craftsy character. And it still valiantly strives to maintain its village aura by eschewing streetlights and house numbers. Many of the houses are constructed in picturesque styles which smack of the kind of architecture usually reserved for illustrations in children's books. With this storyland ambience, it is easy to understand why a Carmel stay was once considered the ideal balm to soothe the psyche, traumatized by modern urban hurly-burly.

As word got around, however, hordes of city dwellers the world over wanted to partake of the Carmel elixir and, in so doing, they changed many of the very qualities they sought. In their frantic rush to escape big-city commercialism and pressure, they created a type of countrified commercialism. During the height of the summer season, Carmel's traffic jams rival in intensity the most clogged city streets. (Traffic ordinances are strict and tightly enforced.) And the once easy-going shop owners who had always welcomed visitors with a smile and had time for a chat, have now taken on a sterner, business-only mien. This also sadly reflects an ideological schizophrenia which seems to infect much of the town. While many Carmelites treat the influx of tourists with disdain and even hostility at times, they cannot survive without the passengers of those thousands of cars which cramp their streets.

Carmel has therefore evolved from the idyllic little village-by-the-sea, into a handsome shopper's mecca, complete with all the problems of overcrowding and commercialism which come hand-in-hand with that kind of "success." And while you still won't find any neon signs on Ocean Avenue or house numbers on the quaint cottages, you will find the latest in international haute-couturier creations, costly antiques, and acres of art. Because I am not enamored with shopping per se, Carmel in this role holds little interest for me.

But . . . Carmel happens to be situated in the heart of one of the most scenically spectacular parts of California, if not the entire United States. And fitted into a four-day trip filled with unrivaled outdoor recreational opportunities, excellent dining, some California history, and the majesty of the most awesome meeting of sea and land in the world, Carmel, in this perspective, with its bevy of smart shops and galleries, is a "must-see."

THE FIRST DAY

With ten championship golf courses (both public and private) and over a dozen tennis clubs (mostly public) in the Carmel-Monterey area, the requisite sports equipment is your first packing consideration. You will also want to take along some comfortable shoes for your shopping forays and for climbing over the more than 300 steps at Hearst's Castle. While Carmel is "country casual" tweedy in dress, men will want to pack a tie for dining in a superb Italian restaurant. The entire area is renowned for its benignly pleasant (although, at times, foggy) climate. So pack accordingly and if you forget to pack something you can always buy it in Carmel—no matter what "it" may be!

10:00 a.m.   After a fine breakfast at Sears' or in your hotel, start off by locating Sixth Street. Head South on

Sixth Street and where it ends drive directly up the entrance ramp to Highway 280. (The most direct route to our destination is to take Highway 101 for about 90 miles before turning off onto Highway 156 for the Monterey Peninsula. Doing so, however, presents an unattractive landscape, tracing the Bay's western perimeter through dull industrial areas for the first 50 some miles. Since this stretch is also the primary commercial avenue to and from San Francisco, and passes the airport, the traffic can be fairly heavy.)

Therefore, I suggest Highway 280, following the signs first to Daly City, then to San Jose. You will first cut through the southern residential portion of San Francisco, then sweep gently up through the hillside bedroom communities of San Mateo County, overlooking the Bay. Soon you will be viewing some lovely hillscapes, with the waters of the Crystal Springs Reservoir glimmering in the sun. Then on through the horse-loving community of Woodside, skirting behind Stanford University and connecting up with 101 just south of San Jose.

Now follow the signs indicating "Highway 101, Los Angeles." This drive takes you through rich farmlands, past prune orchards and grape fields, increasingly threatened by the encroachment of suburban sprawl. Forty-seven miles later, take the turnoff to Highway 156 West, marked "Monterey Peninsula." Suddenly, you will find yourself in the "Artichoke Capital of the World" with acres upon acres of the thistle-like plants stretching to the horizon. Highway 156 then swings into Highway 1 South, which will be the main artery of your travels for the next three days.

Remain on Highway 1 as it by-passes Monterey and do not take any of the Carmel exits. Our destination, the Tickle Pink Motor Inn, is not in Carmel proper but in Carmel Highlands, 4 miles south of Carmel. Watch for a sign on the left indicating the Highlands Inn; then 800 feet later, turn left into its rising driveway, which is marked "Highlands Drive." Continue on up the .drive, passing through the Highlands Inn's parking lot on to the Tickle Pink, right next door.

For over twenty years, the Tickle Pink Motor Inn, 155 Highlands Drive, Carmel, 93923, (408) 624-1244, has been my most favored place to stay while visiting the Carmel-Monterey area. First of all, it perches on a cliffside overlooking the Pacific Ocean, an important advantage over almost all Carmel proper hotels and motels. Each and every room—from the most modest to the lovely suites with functioning stone fireplaces—shares this view. And almost every room has a balcony overlooking the sea, where visitors can savor their morning continental breakfast, presented with the compliments of the inn.

Secondly, I enjoy being removed from the cloyingly "cute" atmosphere of many "downtown" Carmel inns, which make feeble attempts at re-creating English manors and the like. The Tickle Pink is an extremely comfortable, modern motor inn—there is no need for it to try to be something that it isn't. And lastly, in a day and age when housekeeping in tourist-oriented hotels and motels is becoming shockingly poor, the Tickle Pink is scrupulously clean.

Of course, I am not the only traveler who knows of and swears by the Tickle Pink and its enviable charms and comforts. You will, therefore, have to reserve as far in advance as possible. The room charge is somewhat more than the usual run-of-the-mill motel. If you wish to splurge a bit more, ask about their spacious suites, especially those in the new level built about four years ago.

Since the drive down from San Francisco takes anywhere from 2½ to 3 hours, it should now be approaching 1:00 p.m. If you are hungry and would like a bite before starting out on your afternoon, stroll over to the adjacent Highlands Inn. There you will find the California Market (closed Mondays), a mini deli-market where you can buy sandwiches or pates and some fine wines to take back to the Tickle Pink for lunch overlooking the sea. Otherwise, if your breakfast was sufficient, you might wish to wait until dinner.

2:00 p.m. Settled into your Tickle Pink room, it is now time to put your priorities in order—Mother Nature or shopping. If you wish to experience, at close hand, that marvelous meeting of land and sea visible through your picture windows, all you need do is drive about 2 miles back up Highway 1 (toward Carmel) and pull into the Point Lobos State Reserve. Regarded by many as one of the most beautiful pieces of California coast, this 1,500-acre park boasts a 6-mile shoreline, along which you can hike and explore the incredible world of tide pools.

During low tide, these pools are exposed and in them are microcosms of life—starfish, hermit crabs, sea urchins and sea anemones. Squatting by one of the pools and witnessing the beauty within, can mesmerize me for hours.

If, however, you are more enchanted at the moment by man's creations in fashions, art, jewelry, etc., then drive another mile or so beyond Point Lobos to the Ocean Avenue turnoff to the left, which will take you right into the heart of Carmel. Here, you will not require my guidance. What you will need are good walking shoes and a deck of credit cards. Oh, yes, you will also need to find a parking space. If you skipped lunch and are now regretting it, walk over to Patisserie Boissiere on Mission Street, between Ocean and 7th, for tea or coffee and a piece of French pastry.

5:30 p.m. Time to think about returning to the Tickle Pink and enjoying the late afternoon sun over the sparkling Pacific. (If you are in Carmel and wish to take back some cocktail fixings with you, stop in at the superb Mediterranean Market at Ocean and Mission Streets.)

7:30 p.m. Time to head north again, but this time for dinner. Armed with an advance reservation (as usual, I am assuming you have read ahead and have made the necessary telephone call) and with the men in the party dressed in ties (not demanded, but appreciated), head back up Highway 1 toward Carmel. Turn left down

Ocean Avenue to Mission, then right for approximately four blocks to Giuliano's.

Giuliano's, Mission near Fifth, Carmel, (408) 625-5231, (dinner served nightly; lunch Tuesday through Saturday; reservations imperative) is the epitome of a refined Italian restaurant. With its bare white look—only large rust-colored cushions and vases of flowers act as color accents—it is the model of North Italian chic. But far more importantly, its limited menu presents some of the finest Northern Italian dishes in all their glory—not overblown or Frenchified, but with the elegant simplicity that should be the hallmark of fine Italian cuisine.

Therefore, I would splurge both on calories and dollars! Start with an appetizer course split for two: something like their slices of green tomato, lightly breaded and sauteed in olive oil. *Ultimo italiano!* A pasta is a must and the Fettucine alla Giuliano, creamed but not crushed and flavored with two kinds of imported Italian cheeses, is as good as these homemade pasta ribbons get. Or equally outstanding are the Agnolotti, pasta semi-circles filled with unusual stuffings which change daily. They will gladly divide one order between two diners.

Their Picatta di Vitello is also exceptional—thin veal slices are lovingly sauteed to a just-touched-with-brown perfection. Then a soupcon of white wine added to create a slight deglaze which is studded with a few capers and flavored with a squeeze of lemon. Giuliano's sweetbreads further demonstrate the kitchen's restraint. These are simply grilled and kissed with lemon and garlic. Memorable! Vegetables are always fresh and presented on the side, lest they detract from the pristine appearance of the entree plate. On my last visit they were exquisitely done, crunchy Chinese snow peas. which could have been the pride of any Chinese restaurant! For dessert, try one of the made-in-house ice creams: the banana-nut is ambrosial. Or, if you are in luck, they might have on hand their divine Chocolate Cake with a white chocolate sauce. Or their gigantic Profiteroles, filled with some of the home-made ice cream and blanketed in an ebony chocolate sauce. For a wine, have you ever tried that delightful Italian import, Pinot Grigio? Exceptional espresso. Since San Francisco possesses no Italian restaurant of this authentic high style, visiting Carmel without dining at Giuliano's has become an impossibility.

10:30 p.m. Before you return to the Tickle Pink, you might wish to stroll along the now nearly deserted streets of Carmel. In the vicinity of Giuliano's, watch your step; Carmel still shuns the urban conveniences of paved sidewalks and curbs. Along Ocean Avenue, though, your eyes can focus on the shop windows without distraction. You might relish an after-dinner brandy at the bar in the Pine Inn on Ocean Avenue before heading back down Highway 1 to a sleep softly lulled by the sound of the ocean surf.

THE SECOND DAY

8:00 a.m. This is the earliest hour at which you can receive your complimentary continental breakfast at the Tickle Pink. You may have to forgo it if golf is your game and you want to get out early. If golf is not your game, it certainly is the game of the Carmel-Monterey Peninsula which sports the title "Golf Capital of the World." You may never have held a putter in your hands, but it is almost certain you have seen photos of the incredible 16th hole at Cypress Point, 220 yards of blue Pacific between tee and green. Tennis is another favored recreation here and the area is dotted with courts. To ensure either golf or tennis availability, it is best to check with your travel agent or golf and tennis clubs at home.

If you do not wish to spend this morning on the greens or the courts, I have a few suggestions. If you spent yesterday afternoon at Point Lobos, perhaps you are ready to poke around Carmel's shops this morning. Or, you might take a journey back in time to the beginnings of Carmel by visiting the mission officially known as the Basilica San Carlos Borromeo del Rio Carmelo. To reach this historic link with California's past and the final resting place of Father Junipero Serra, the founder of California's chain of missions, drive north toward Carmel, taking the Rio Road turnoff to the left. Or, you might wish to just beachcomb along the sandy Carmel beach, depending on what the fog is doing. If you do go, take your camera along to capture the photogenic wind-tortured cypress trees.

About now, you should give some consideration to where or rather, how you wish to lunch. As usual, I have a couple of recommendations. The first is a picnic along the north shore of the famed 17-Mile Drive; the second, a fine garden restaurant in the neighboring city of Monterey, where you should spend the afternoon. Whatever your choice, start off by heading back to Ocean Avenue in Carmel.

11:00 a.m.   Drive down Ocean Avenue. (If you opted for the picnic, purchase whatever provisions you desire at either the Mediterranean in the heart of Carmel or at the California Market next door at the Highlands Inn. And don't forget some pastries from Patisserie Boissiere.) Proceed down Ocean Avenue until you just about reach the beach, turning right at the "17-Mile Drive" sign. Pass through the gate (a $5.00 per auto charge for non-residents); ask for a map; and take the first left, ignoring the "17-Mile Drive" marker. Then pick up the red-dashed center line, marking your course through the drive.

Actually, you will only be traversing about half of the entire 17 miles, but it is by far the most scenic half. Within minutes, the famed Pebble Beach Golf Links will be on your left. (By the way, the Club XIX at the Lodge serves quite good lunches from tables overlooking the 18th hole and the Pacific beyond.) Ranked in the top 10, this course serves as the home of the AT&T (formerly the Bing Crosby) Pro-Am Tournament each January. Then you will cut through an exclusive colony of mansions, erected in every imaginable style from Moorish to Modern to Colonial, yet they all have one thing in common—great wealth. Out on a wind-swept point you will view "Lone

Cypress," possibly the most painted and photographed tree in all America. Then comes the Cypress Point Club (private) and Fanshell Beach, a crescent of white sand where you can enjoy your picnic. Just a little further on (an ideal after-lunch walk), you will come upon Seal and Bird Rocks, the habitat of shore birds, sea lions and sea otters. Whatever you do, stop here for a few minutes to watch and listen to the hordes of sea lions on the offshore rocks.

Continuing on the 17-Mile Drive, watch for the sign marked "Pacific Grove Gate" and turn left. Soon you will exit the toll portion of the Drive and as you continue ahead the 17-Mile Drive becomes an ordinary quiet suburban street.

If the time of your visit happens to be in October or early November, I urge you to turn right onto Pine Street for two blocks. For on the corner of Grove Street and Pine is a small grove of trees which serve as the winter home of the monarch butterflies; enormous clusters of them are best visible in the afternoon sun. Otherwise, continue along the 17-Mile Drive to Lighthouse Avenue, turn right and you will soon find yourself in the heart of Pacific Grove, a delightfully Victorian seaside town, founded by the Methodists over 100 years ago as a site for camp meetings.

Now proceed down Lighthouse Avenue to David, then left downhill to famed Cannery Row. Though immortalized by John Steinbeck as "a poem, a stink, a grating noise," today those attributes have all but vanished. Almost all the ancient, weather-worn canneries have been converted into modern warrens of shops, restaurants, art galleries, etc. Tourists pack them as tightly as their previous occupants—the sardines!

However, at the foot of David Street, on your left you will find the Monterey Bay Aquarium. Even if you do not particularly like zoos or aquariums, I urge you not to miss this spectacular exhibit. So you should stop and see if they have any tickets available during your stay, unless you have made prior arrangements, which are certainly advisable. You see, since it opened in late 1984, the Monterey Bay Aquarium has become one of California's most popular attractions and tickets usually must be ordered in advance. However, again assuming you are reading ahead, let me fill you in on how you can experience this incredible structure.

Tickets should be purchased more than seven days in advance through Ticketron by calling 392-SHOW or visiting one of their outlets in The Emporium on Market Street between Fourth and Fifth Streets or by writing to them at P.O. Box 26430, San Francisco, CA 94126. Tickets are $7 for adults; $3 for children age 3-12; $5 for seniors. There is also a $1 per ticket service charge.

What was once an old fish canning factory has been transformed into a miraculous display of marine life, not in the usual tiny porthole-sized viewing chambers, but in towering sea-life galleries. Here the visitor has an eye-to-eye view of nearly 5,000 creatures that live in Monterey Bay. Children will especially love the hands-on exhibits where they can touch starfish and even bat rays.

On my first visit, I thought I would do a cursory run-through just to see if I should recommend it to you. Over two hours later I emerged absolutely exhilarated. In fact, if you plan to visit the Aquarium, I would amend my agenda a bit and see it before visiting the Point Lobos State Reserve. In this way a tour of the Aquarium is like a preliminary course preparing you for what you will later see in all its full natural splendor.

Right now we will proceed down Cannery Row, hugging the waterfront. Soon Cannery Row turns right into Drake St. Continue up Drake to Lighthouse, where you turn left. Lighthouse Ave. will take you through the Military Reserve and, via a tunnel, into downtown Monterey. Emerging from the tunnel, make a right onto Tyler, then left onto Franklin and, one block later, turn right onto Washington which soon becomes Abrego. On your left, at number 565, a small clock tower marks the luncheon restaurant for those who preferred not to picnic. Locate a parking spot nearby. Even if you are not planning to lunch here, this is a good place from which to begin a walking tour of Old Monterey, the former capital of California and one of the most historic cities in the state. But first, for those who will now enter its gates, a bit about The Clock Garden, 565 Abrego, Monterey, (408) 375-6100, (open daily for lunch and dinner).

Lunching in the garden of The Clock Garden is like dining in an outdoor nursery in riotous full bloom. The brick patio is alive with potted flowering geraniums and daisies and the thick, plank tables also support pots of growing plants. If consummate care has been lavished in providing a delightfully relaxed, sunny atmosphere, the same infinite attention has been paid to the short yet refreshingly simple menu. Superb homemade soups can act as the opening course or the main attraction, chaperoned by bread and a mini salad. Only one soup is featured each day, but you can bank on its unerring excellence, be it the delicious Clam Chowder or the velvety, egg-thickened Greek Lemon.

The Garden Salad—almost an entire head of crisp lettuce, topped with a wealth of ham, turkey, cheese and countless other goodies—is barely contained in its enormous bowl. The toothsome dressing is thoughtfully served on the side so diners can employ their own discretion in its application. For hot dishes, the Crepes Carlotta are sure-fire winners. After the cardboard "crepes" of franchised creperies, it is rewarding indeed to come across real, truly flavorful crepes, golden and rich. A haunting mixture of spinach, turkey and cheese, heightened by a touch of what I believe is cumin, is enveloped within them. Totally delightful! If salmon is in season, the Cold Poached Salmon is faultless in both quality and execution, partnered by a dilled Cucumber Salad. Sandwiches are heartily abundant and the Pecan Pie is my dessert choice. By looking around you at the people who crowd inside the charming garden, you can plainly see that The Clock Garden is not just another "tourist restaurant," but one that local residents cherish, just as I do and, I daresay, you will.

Whether or not you lunch at The Clock Garden, it is a fine spot from which to begin a small walking tour of Old Monterey. (The visitor's free monthly magazine, *This Month*, usually prints the route of a historic walking tour in each issue which you can use as a handy guide.)

You can start out by turning right as you exit The Clock Garden's gate, then left on Pearl Street where you can pick up the walking tour by keeping an eye on the dark red stripe on the roadbed. During this walk you will pass several historic adobes, many dating from 1830, including the Stevenson House, once the home of Robert Louis Stevenson which contains a collection of memorabilia dating to 1879. Local Stevenson scholars like to point out that the geography of Point Lobos is remarkably similar to that of Stevenson's fictional *Treasure Island*.

Also along the walk you will come upon the Larkin House (daily guided tours), a perfect example of the "Monterey style" of architecture which had its beginnings as Spanish adobe (early 1800's) but was later modified by the New England seamen with the addition of a second story and a balcony. Colton Hall on Pacific Street, built in 1847-49, is possibly the finest of the remaining old buildings. Other interesting structures along the route are the Custom House, the oldest government building on the Pacific Coast; and California's First Theater (1846-1847) with its display of theatrical souvenirs from the past.

How much time you spend viewing and visiting these historic buildings depends upon your interest and perhaps the weather. If it is a fine day, this walk is an extremely pleasant way to assimilate some history while enjoying the sun. When you have soaked up enough of both, simply find your way back to Abrego Street and your car. To return to the Tickle Pink, continue out Abrego, which merges into Munras, which brings you right to Highway 1 South.

6:00 p.m. Your last night in Carmel might start out with cocktails again on your Tickle Pink deck, or in the beautiful Pacific's Edge Room of the Highlands Inn next door. But allow at least twenty minutes driving-and-parking time to reach our dinner destination for this evening—The Whaling Station, 763 Wave Street near Cannery Row, Monterey, (408) 373-4248, (open nightly; reservations advised).

Also, because you must drive through downtown Monterey, which has a large number of one-way streets, it is advised you allow plenty of time for wrong turns. Drive north on Highway 1, passing Carmel to the Munras turnoff. Keep on Munras, then onto Alvarado to Del Monte. Left on Del Monte two blocks to Pacific, and right on Pacific, picking up signs to Cannery Row.

8:30 p.m. The Whaling Station succeeds primarily because the owners do not suffer from "overreach," a malady fatal to so many restaurants. Here overriding emphasis is on fresh fish, simply prepared. Now, most fish restaurants claim that is their goal, too. What makes the Whaling Station different is that they stick to their word. They don't augment their menu with a freezer chest of frozen seafood, even when the weather prevents the fishing fleet from bringing in the catch! And they show style in a number of other ways.

The moment you are seated you are presented with *the* vegetable of the area—a beautifully cooked, cold artichoke, in its center an herbed mayonnaise and a vinaigrette. Soups tend to be handsomely executed with some type of fish chowder usually on the stove. Then comes your choice of a fresh fish, grilled over oakwood and mesquite charcoal. Also, here is the place to encounter that now elusive mollusk, the abalone. I ask for it breaded and also request that the superfluous sprinkling of grated cheese be omitted. Vegetables are always fresh and often offbeat, such as the sprightly dandelion greens served one evening. For dessert try their Canoli, that deep-fried tube encasing a rich, sweetened ricotta cheese mixture. Service is fleet, the young staff displaying far more seafood savvy than many of their more seasoned San Francisco confreres. The wine list is unusually strong on smaller California vintners with a special section devoted to wines of

Monterey County. In all, The Whaling Station is the kind of seafood house San Francisco should have more of— especially on our Fisherman's Wharf! Moderate prices for excellent food and service in an atmosphere aglow with good vibes.

10:00 p.m.   Better head back to your motel, you have a long drive tomorrow.

THE THIRD DAY

Your last chance to get in a morning of golf or tennis, or to make up your mind if that seascape painting you spotted in that Carmel side-street gallery would really suit the den wall. Then, it is packing and setting off down the coast.

Perhaps on your numerous treks back and forth from Carmel and Monterey to the Tickle Pink, you may have noticed a rather ominous sign on the roadside heading south reading: "Curves and hills next 74 miles." To those unaccustomed to California's coastal terrain, I want to impress upon you just what that means. It means that Highway 1, your approach to Hearst's Castle at San Simeon, will be at most times a two-lane roller coaster, clinging precariously to the sheer sides of the Santa Lucia Mountains with only a few feet of gravel and perhaps a low stone wall between you and the Pacific Ocean a couple hundred feet below. Even though I have covered this stretch many times, I would not traverse it in fog, rain or dark of night. I certainly do not want to frighten you out of this important leg of your trip because the rewards in unique scenery and Hearst's Castle are well worth the effort. But you should be aware of what lies ahead.

11:00 a.m.   All packed, you now exit from the Tickle Pink, turning left onto Highway 1. Our lunch destination (about 25 miles south) can be reached in 40 minutes, so you have plenty of time to take it easy, pulling onto some of the numerous turnouts on the right to better contemplate the vast panorama. Words fail to accurately describe this powerful meeting of land mass and surging sea—a symphony in itself which is called Big Sur Country.

12:00 noon. By this time, you should be at Nepenthe, (408) 667-2345, (open daily for lunch and dinner) where you will be having lunch. Aptly named after the mythical drug which possessed the magical power to induce forgetfulness of sorrow, Nepenthe is far more than just a place to eat—it is a state of mind. The moment I arrive, my mind immediately casts off "city concerns" and begins to quietly flow with the sweep of the mountains that curve into the sea. Here, 800 feet above the Pacific, you are in another world, one without worries, one that is an extension of nature. The restaurant blends into its environment with its use of bare beams and adobe. The original building was the honeymoon cottage Orson Welles built for his bride, Rita Hayworth, in the '40s. And although the structure has been expanded greatly and now includes a two-story gift-and-handicraft shop, the entire complex remains totally unobtrusive and completely natural.

The food Nepenthe serves is created in the same vein. Simplicity is the keynote, and the finest quality is the accepted norm. As you laze on the outside terrace overlooking the massive coastline to the south, you will swear your Ambrosia Burger is the finest you have ever enjoyed. The kosher pickle crackles under your bite and the bean salad beams with sprightly herbs. French fries must be ordered separately and are cooked to order. I regard them as the ultimate in fries—crispy, golden and irresistible. And what a delight to find tea (no tea bag, either!) as beautifully brewed as it would be in a Mayfair drawing room. Sit here awhile and sip in silence. Nepenthe is to be slowly savored. It is a unique place.

1:45 p.m. I am always loathe to leave Nepenthe, to quit its hold on my senses, to take leave of the peaceful aura radiated by the Big Sur regulars who gather here, using it as a social and cultural center. But . . . we must leave.

We are headed to one of the most mind-boggling displays of ostentatious power and wealth in America. The drive to Hearst's Castle proper covers less than 60 miles, most of it being curves and hills. It should take over 2 hours, depending on stops. Speaking of stops, an important one for those interested in the creativity of the Big Sur Colony, is the Coast Gallery, south of Nepenthe on the left.

As you approach San Simeon, you can spot the massive complex of buildings on the crest of a hill several miles off in the distance, looming above the countryside like some wild creation of mad King Ludwig of Bavaria. Your overnight lodgings lie about 6½ miles further south, but you may wish to pull into the Castle's tourist center in order to pick up a brochure on the history and contents of the place.

The best way to avoid finding that tours to the Castle are all sold out on the day you arrive is to purchase your tickets in San Francisco before departing for San Simeon. Tickets for any of the three different major tours (see below for descriptions) are available through Ticketron, Inc. (392-SHOW) or from any one of their outlets, such as the one in the Emporium, Market Street between Fourth and Fifth Streets, or in most Tower and Rainbow Record stores as well as at various other locations in the Bay Area. Ticketron tacks on a nominal service charge, which is a small price to pay for the convenience and protection against disappointment.

Failing to obtain your Hearst Castle tickets in San Francisco, you should purchase them at the Castle on the afternoon of your arrival for the earliest available tours the next morning.

As of this writing, there are actually four tours available. All tours are guided. No cars are allowed up at the Castle; you are bused there. Tour #1 includes the swimming pools, one guest house, the garden, and the ground floor of the Castle itself. Tour #2 shows you the pools, garden, upper level of the Castle and the kitchen. Tour #3 takes in the pools, garden and guest rooms of the

North Wing. Tour #4 is a personally guided private tour for small groups. It lasts about 4 to 4½ hours and is available by appointment only.

Tour #1 is the one I recommend for all first-time visitors, but I have found some of the rooms on Tour #2 extremely interesting, especially the Celestial Suite filled with an almost magical light created by the sun filtering through the filligree-carved shutters. Naturally, the kitchen holds a special place in my interests!

There is little reason for me to devote much time to details on the Castle or its contents. The complimentary brochure and your well-schooled guides will give you plenty of facts and figures. All I can and should say is that you are due for an intriguing experience. I had thought from my reading that all of it was grotesque and in poor taste. So I was in for a surprise when I first visited it.

Here are some magnificent antiques, even if intermixed with little regard for their aesthetic effect on one another, to say nothing of an utter disregard for chronology.

The most surprising thing, however, is that the Castle was not created as a stuffy museum but as the actual, comfortable residence of one man. I think this is the thing which astonishes tourists. Big, overstuffed, inexpensive and floral-covered chairs are scattered in rooms containing ceilings worth hundreds of thousands of dollars. This, too, comes up for much criticism on the part of interior decorators, but I do not agree. One must keep in mind that floral, overstuffed chairs were much in vogue in the days this Castle was being furnished and, whether they are in good taste or not, they certainly look comfortable and inviting. In fact, all the rooms look livable despite the inclusion of some startling antique pieces.

A trip to Hearst's Castle would be worth it for the outdoor swimming pool alone. I doubt if you will ever see anything like this again in American architecture. It is breathtakingly beautiful. Add to this the great variety of flowers and fruit trees which, incidentally, are especially magnificent in the spring, and you will have a two-hour tour you will never forget.

After stopping at the Castle's tourist center to pick up an illustrated brochure, simply continue further down Highway 1 for 6½ miles to Moonstone Beach Drive, turning right to San Simeon Pines, (805) 927-4648. The Pines is by no means elegant or luxurious, but it is perfect for your one-night stay. The whole atmosphere is friendly and accommodating. An even greater plus is the fact that only a few yards away is a lovely seashore park, maintained by the state. Here you can shuffle aimlessly along the sandy beach, or sit up on the bluff among the cypress awaiting the descent of the sun into the vast Pacific. It is an ideal place to stretch your legs after the tension of the Highway 1 drive. (Closer to the Castle is the larger, more modern and box-like San Simeon Lodge, 805-927-4601.)

When you check into the Pines, ask the clerk to place a dinner reservation for you at whatever hour you wish at the Brambles, Burton Drive, Cambria, (805) 927-4716, (open nightly for dinner; reservations advised). The Brambles is the kind of restaurant one hopes to uncover in out-of-the-way tourist spots, but seldom does. After all, here is an establishment catering primarily to one-time Castle visitors. The majority of restaurants which have this kind of captive, never-to-return clientele usually take advantage of the situation with poor food and service. Happily for you, the Brambles is a noteworthy exception. The menu is the plain, honest-to-goodness type with no frills. But the steaks and salmon (in season) are broiled to perfection over oak coals. The Clam Chowder is unusually tasty, and the breads are homemade. On one visit, both the onion bread and light-textured pumpernickel were delicious. If a restaurant takes the time and trouble to bake their own breads, one would expect out-of-the-ordinary baked desserts—and the Brambles' cheesecake was just that. Faultlessly swift and efficient service in this remote area makes me wonder all the more why so many city restaurants cannot come up with the same.

THE FOURTH DAY

Hopefully, you were able to purchase tickets to a fairly early morning tour of the Castle. So the best course of action is to pack up the car first, check out and head north to the Castle.

After you have witnessed Mr. Hearst's home and pondered a bit on the unfathomable wealth that allowed him to construct it, you are ready to end your excursion and to return to San Francisco. You do not have to face tortuous Highway 1 again. There is a very simple route back. It will not give you the incredible scenic wonders of the Big Sur Coast, but its straight four-lane freeway construction certainly will be welcomed.

All you need do is exit left from the Castle's parking area, heading south on Highway 1. In 12½ miles, turn left again on Highway 46.

After 20 miles of smooth, gradually graded roadway rising to some 1,700 feet above verdant farmlands, you will connect with Highway 101 North. In about 3½ to 4 hours, you will be back in San Francisco. However, the first one who says, "That Hearst Castle is a great place to visit, but I wouldn't want to live there" walks!

If, after your long drive back to San Francisco, you want to just settle for a room-service dinner in your hotel, I can't really blame you. I know the feeling all too well! On the other hand, because there was no scheduled lunch stop, a visit to another fine restaurant might be just the thing after a brief rest. And to fill that bill, I have two recommendations.

The Peacock, 2800 Van Ness Avenue at Lombard (928-7001; dinner served nightly; lunch served daily except Saturday; reservations), is just one of three superior Indian restaurants now in San Francisco. Yet, for many years the city could not boast of a single first-class Indian dining room. So when the estimable Gaylord, of the international chain, opened in Ghirardelli Square, curry connoisseurs welcomed it with enthusiasm. And it was immediately included in previous editions of this guide. No doubt encouraged by Gaylord's success, The

Peacock soon appeared in a beautifully renovated stately old house just a few blocks away. And then with the construction of Davies Hall and the transformation of the Civic Center into a performing arts center, the Kundan opened in Opera Plaza which is further down Van Ness Avenue.

Actually, I would recommend all three of these establishments without hesitation. However, I selected Peacock for this edition because of a couple extra-plus factors. First of all, you dine in the high-ceilinged rooms of an old residence, redone in warm apricot and serene white. Secondly, for those unversed in Indian cuisine, Peacock offers a beautifully constructed complete dinner, the Shaan-e-Mayur, which showcases some of their finest dishes.

But before we begin this complete dinner, let's have a Pimm's Cup along with an a la carte order of Vegetable Pokoras, sort of an Indian tempura. Then, onto the dinner proper, beginning with Tandoori Murgh. Here is chicken to sigh over, marinated in yoghurt and spices and cooked in an ultra-hot clay oven, a tandoor, to a crisped-skin yet succulent perfection. From the same Punjab oven also emerges your Boti Kebab, cubes of spiced lamb. Served with these is one of the great breads of Indian cuisine, Masala Kulcha, an herb and onion-speckled leavened flat bread.

For your next course you are presented with three of Peacock's finest curried dishes. Actually the word "curry" never appears on the Peacock menu. By shunning the term, they attempt to call attention to the vast variety of spice combinations and marriages too often lumped haphazardly under this umbrella term. As you sample each, take a moment to allow each flavor picture to fully focus, before you proceed on to the next. There is Rogan Josh Kashmiri, a dish of braised lamb in a fragrant tomato-vegetable mixture; Baingan Bharta, intriguing charcoal baked eggplant; and Murgh Sagwala, chicken with spiced spinach. All three are "curry" dishes, yet each has its own unique flavor achieved by its own individual blend of spices. Served with these three dishes is a saffron-scented rice, Mattar Pillau. Dinner concludes with your choice of Indian desserts and, of course, tea.

Given the lovely subdued atmosphere, the thoughtfulness inherent in this complete dinner, the expertise of execution and the very moderate price (about $20), The Peacock proudly presents to both novices and cognoscenti of Indian cuisine a dinner to savor. (Oh yes, a complete vegetarian dinner is also available.)

Pierre, Meridien Hotel, 50 Third Street off Market (974-6400; open nightly except Sunday for dinner; Monday through Friday for lunch; reservations advised) could not have gotten off to a worse start when it debuted a few years ago. For openers, the outward appearance of the new Meridien Hotel was denounced by just about every San Franciscan. And Alain Chapel, one of France's top chefs who planned the menu and can perform miracles in the kitchen, apparently is not as adept at public relations. And some of his statements were construed to belittle existing San Francisco restaurants. But the *coup de grace* was that the opening menu was disastrously executed by the Chapel-trained staff.

Now that the dust has cleared, and a new executive chef is in charge under Chapel's direction, the Pierre has risen Phoenix-like from the ashes of its opening debacle to become one of the city's finest French restaurants. And although, as of this moment, it can still more finely hone its service—unneccesary waits to be seated are the unfortunate rule—its kitchen can afford you a heady venture into the rarefied atmosphere of exciting *nouvelle cuisine*, provided you can afford the tariff.

For example, a salad composed of warm thinly sliced and lightly sauteed sweetbreads, avocado and pink grapefruit is culinary legerdemain. While a simple terrine of duck liver is sheer velvet of the highest quality. A fricassee of scallops and crayfish wears a robe of the lightest of cream sauces, chastely kissed by the merest whisper of tarragon.

A breathtakingly underdone pigeon has a crackly skin,

glazed with honey and lime. And surrounding it are a troop of tiny artichokes the size of your thumb and the smallest of new potatoes. At times, however, I think Chapel's inventiveness goes a tad beyond my comprehension with combinations like a heavenly tender veal, served with a puzzling eggplant sauce. However, the spinach ravioli which come along for the ride are joyous.

When you dine out as often as I do, there are some dishes which refuse to leave your palate memory for months. Such is the indelible flavor of the passionfruit pie. Should you wish something less exotic, the fresh raspberries are of impeccable quality and the cream custard beneath them sheer bliss. A carefully groomed but not copious wine list includes some excellent, moderately priced wines selected by Chapel himself. As with Sutter 500, whose cuisine is overseen by another French great, Roger Verge, Pierre offers the San Francisco a cuisine the likes of which is nigh impossible to discover outside Chapel's bastion in France. Top dollar, but then you save on the air fare of flying to France.

NOTE: To those readers who are visiting San Francisco while attending a convention or meeting at Moscone Center, Pierre is certainly the nearest fine restaurant. So if that sales rep pressing you to sign that six-figure deal asks where you would like to lunch, suggest Pierre in the Meridien.

A Three-Day Trip

to the Napa Valley

NOTE: The Sixth Day's schedule is a day's outing to the wine country, which covers some of the same area as this recommended three-day trip. Therefore, you may wish to refer to it, when making plans for this more extended visit.

Twenty-five years ago when the very first edition of this book saw printer's ink, I would never have thought of including an overnight stay in the beautiful Napa Valley, California's most famous wine-producing area. The reason was simple: there were no really fine places to spend the night and even good, let alone great, dining spots were non-existent.

But now, that has all changed. Today, the Napa Valley can provide all kinds of accommodations from dozens of bed-and-breakfast nooks to a few deluxe resorts. And as for restaurants, the Valley now boasts of some that can rival the finest in San Francisco.

Actually I doubt if there is any one single factor that can claim the distinction—dubious to many who loved the Valley's more peaceful former mein—of placing the Napa Valley high on the list of places for both local resident and tourist to visit. Perhaps the gasoline crunch of several years ago made localites finally realize that the Valley offered the peace, quiet and guaranteed warm summer days, which had made far more distant Lake Tahoe such a haven for generations.

And then there was television. When *Falconcrest* became a hit series, millions upon millions of Americans became aware of the Napa Valley and a lot of them wanted to see it and the actual Falconcrest house.

Well, while I have never seen *Falconcrest*—neither the TV show nor the actual house—I too have become a regular Napa Valley goer. But my reasons are that it offers me dual pleasures—a wonderful place to relax and the opportunity to dine splendidly—all within the reach of a tankful of gas.

But what about you? Should you plan a stay of a day or two in the Napa Valley? Well, do you like hot summer days which offer nothing more exciting than time to laze around a pool or visit some of the greatest wineries in America? Do you enjoy the rural sights of a breathtakingly beautiful valley covered with mile upon mile of vines? Would you relish dining in small country restaurants—like those you thought existed only in France—which serve some of the most elevated *haute cuisine* in the West?

Well, if you answered yes to any or all of the above, then you should plan a two-night stay in the Napa Valley.

But just where do you stay?

I have personally bedded down at three of the best known inns in the Valley. And rather than simply recommend one, I will tell you about all three and you can make up your own mind.

Auberge du Soleil, 180 Rutherford Hill Road, Rutherford, (707) 963-1211, certainly heads the list as the most luxurious. Situated in an olive grove on a hillside, the inn offers a view of the valley from each of its 36 rooms and suites. Each also has a wet bar, fireplace and deck, from where on early mornings you can watch majestic multicolored hot-air balloons drift lazily over the valley. (Ballooning is a big attraction in the Napa Valley, but more about that later.) The decor of the rooms, especially the living areas of the suites, is superb. The inn also has a small but beautifully situated swimming pool as well as tennis courts and a sauna. My preference in rooms or a suite are those on the top floor of the lower terrace, such as the Lorraine (each is named after a province of France). But we are talking top dollar when we speak of the

Auberge du Soleil. And I can heartily recommend everything about this beautiful "Inn of the Sun" except . . . the restaurant.

Sad to say, on my last visit I found the cuisine an extreme disappointment. Meaningless melanges of ingredients were the rule—a sort of *nouvelle cuisine* version of the dartboard school of cooking I abhor. Overreach was pitifully obvious, producing a parade of overindulgent and misunderstood attempts to emulate the unique creations of the Auberge's original master chef, Masa Kobayashi. It does his memory a disservice. I hope by the time you read these words, both the management and the kitchen will have realized the error of their ways and made sweeping changes.

Therefore, if you stay at the Auberge, you might wish to try lunch to see if matters have improved in the kitchen since this unhappy experience. With such stunningly appointed accommodations in the best vantage point overlooking the valley, the Auberge du Soleil should have an equally impressive cuisine.

The Wine Country Inn, 1152 Lodi Lane, St. Helena, (707) 963-7077, is the place to stay if you like real country-inn ambience. Located further north up the valley on a gentle slope, the inn looks as if it has been there for years. But it hasn't. It was just built to look that way. Inside the rooms are cozy with bright patterned materials used in profusion and pretty but not spectacular rural views. They are far removed from the trendy "decorated" rooms of the Auberge du Soleil. And don't bother to look for a phone or a TV set in the room, there is none. One concession to modern tastes is being installed in the Spring of 1986, when a swimming pool is supposed to reach completion. There is no restaurant, but complimentary continental breakfasts are served in the homey public room. An ideal spot for those who really like to get away.

The Vintage Inn, Yountville, (707) 944-1112 or toll free 800-9-VALLEY, is the newest of the three deluxe places to stay, having opened in the Fall of 1985. It seems as though the designers were quite conscious of its prosaic location—right between the highway and the main street of Yountville—and tried to distract from that disadvantage with some very clever ploys. For example, a long artificial stream features several small fountains, their pleasant splash making you less aware of the traffic sounds from the very nearby main road. The rooms are lavishly appointed in soothing colors, often incorporating shades of wine tones. Each has a fireplace and whirlpool bathtub. A plentiful continental breakfast with champagne is served in the public area, while there is a chilled bottle of wine in your room's refrigerator. The help is youthful and aims to please. But even with all this attention to detail, The Vintage Inn still seems to me to be a large motel, albeit a very comfortable, handsomely appointed and well designed one.

So with advance reservations at one of these establishments or at some other place you have heard of, let's not waste any further time but get going.

Although it is a bit circuitous, one of the best ways to reach the Napa Valley is to follow my directions to reach the Valley of the Moon, another wine-producing area which runs parallel to the Napa Valley. You will find full details in Day Six of this book. Basically this route takes you across the Golden Gate Bridge, up through Marin County and on to the town of Sonoma. Here you can either picnic at a nearby winery or lunch at the superb Au Relais. Then drive up the Valley of the Moon, taking the Oakville Grade to cross over into the Napa Valley. The Oakville Grade ends at Highway 29, the main thoroughfare of the Napa Valley, from which you can easily find your inn for the night within a few minutes.

As I said at the beginning of this chapter, there is very little to do in the Napa Valley except relax, so I will depart from my usual hour-by-hour agenda and simply make some general suggestions for activities but some very specific ones for dining. Let's start on a place to dine for tonight.

I hope you like French cuisine because that's definitely the best kind practiced up here. And it can be absolutely superb—provided you know where to go. And here are my two favorite places to dine—provided you have made reservations far in advance.

Miramonte, 1327 Railroad Avenue, St. Helena, (707) 963-3970; dinner served Wednesday through Sunday; no credit cards; reservations essential as far in advance as possible. This is arguably the finest restaurant in the Napa Valley. Chef Udo Nechutny has a phenomenal way with flavors and textures. Unfortunately, just about everybody shares this opinion and Miramonte is packed to the rafters, which resound with decibel levels that OSHA would probably find hazardous to your health. It is a shame because the noise can distract from the truly superb cuisine. Distract it might, but it doesn't deter me from visiting Miramonte religiously on every visit to the Valley.

The menu always consists of two set dinners. Even though it is handwritten anew each day, there are invariably a host of unlisted dishes. This necessitates the waiter's having to recite a descriptive litany over the already numbing hubbub. A very disconcerting arrangement.

Since the menu changes constantly, here are some of the types of creations you can expect. Japanese eggplant done Provencale style with fresh tomatoes and tiny black olives. An artichoke bottom cooked to utter perfection in a creamy vinaigrette. Fresh reed-thin asparagus bathed in a mousseline of such pristine creaminess and delicacy that you believe you never want to taste another mousseline again, knowing it will fail in comparison. Couquille St. Jacques—with the roe intact—in a seamless cream sauce. Lamb tongue in a matchless vinaigrette. A filet mignon in a fathoms-deep burgundy sauce. Rack of lamb in two sauces, one of yoghurt that I thought would be impossible but somehow with Udo's wizardry works.

A tempting, palate-cleansing light salad follows, then desserts—the likes of three small profiteroles, each with a different filling and topping. Remarkable local wines and some imports (a rarity in the chauvinistic Napa Valley). Expensive—but worth it for some of the finest French cuisine in Northern California.

Le Rhone, 1234 Main Street, St. Helena, (707) 963-0240; dinner served Wednesday through Sunday; no credit cards; reservations imperative. Even though Le Rhone is one of the Napa Valley's newer arrivals, I have known its cuisine for many years, because George and Eliane Chalaye have operated a couple of restaurants previously in the Bay Area. Then after spending some time back in their native France, they returned to open Le Rhone in the Napa Valley. My fervent wish is that they will now stay put and continue to offer their superb specialties, many from the Rhone Valley.

Dinner at Le Rhone is fixed-price affair but you are given some choice in each course. For openers, you might be tempted by juniper-scented pieces of tender rabbit surrounded by a fresh tomato coulis. Or the most ambrosial duck liver mousse with a fascinating peppery gelee. Or a gelee of duck stock afloat in a ruby-red beet soup. For a main course, domestic venison with a champion Grand Veneur sauce is unsurpassable. Yet, the ultimate mignon of lamb must be considered. Rather than mishandling a wealth of different vegetables for different entrees, Le Rhone comes up with something like a haunting puree of celery root or a timbale of spinach along with their fine, although at times a tad too garlicky, pommes dauphinoise.

And if you are a dessert fancier, you have just passed through the Pearly Gates. Years ago when Mimi Sheraton called from New York to ask which San Francisco restaurant had the finest desserts, Jack Shelton and I did not hesitate a moment in naming Le Rhone. And they keep up that high-calorie tradition with carts of mousses, cakes, fruit tarts, sauces, etc. You can even create your own fanatasy by combining several. Mme. Chalaye appears positively crestfallen if you don't gorge yourself! Absolute Lucullan cuisine!

I realize that after dinners like either of the ones above, the last thing you want to think about is food. But let me give you a couple of lunch recommendations. I won't bother with breakfast, since all three of my recommended places to stay offer complimentary continental breakfasts which should suffice.

Mount View Hotel, 1457 Lincoln Avenue, Calistoga, (707) 942-6877. Lunch is served daily, except Sunday when a brunch is served; dinner nightly. A visit to this old hotel on the main drag of sleepy Calistoga is a must for those who relish art deco. The bar off the small lobby looks like a Hollywood set onto which Fred and Ginger will soon tap, perhaps leaping from one high-gloss table to another. The whole hotel toasts the '20s, including the dining room which contains walls of ads and prints from the roaring decade.

From the menu you could start with a serving of two house pates—a liver pate of pure velure and a coarser country cousin, emboldened with orange rind. Meaux mustard (that seedy new darling of trendy menus), cornichons, capers and chopped onions chaperone. For a main course, a homemade fettucine with bacon, tomato and fresh basil is the right respite from our French dining marathon. And this is no "tomato sauce" but rather pieces of freshly stewed tomato to which the other ingredients have been added at the last moment. Delicious. The sauteed chicken is equally ingratiating, with its light tarragon-touched cream sauce served with perfectly steamed brocolli. If you wish to skip dessert—although the chocolate cake with a creme anglaise is bewitching— you might wish to opt for a Pecota Muscat Andrea, a local dessert wine of distinction.

Mustards Grill, 7339 St. Helena Highway just north of Yountville, (707) 944-2424; open daily for lunch and dinner; reservations best. The minute you walk into this roadside grill you are greeted by an almost tangible sense of excitement. It is not just that the place will be crowded— it always is—but it just gives out good vibes. The room is attractive in a lean-clean way with dulcet pastel art on the walls. If you have heard of California cuisine and wondered what it was, just glance at that menu. There you will find plenty of references to goat cheese, mesquite

grilling, sun-dried tomatoes and homemade mustards—
all essentials in the California cooking of the late '80s.

A string bean salad of blushingly young, raw *haricot
verts* is tossed with smoked tomato and crumbled goat
cheese and garnished with fingers of endive. The smoked
beef tenderloin resembles Italian carpaccio—razor-thin
almost raw beef on which a light mustard has been
dribbled. The calf's liver is creamy textured and the
accompanying carmelized onions mouthwatering. But
don't miss the angelhair onion rings or the new potatoes,
simply grilled skins and all. Delicious grilled quail and
one of the West's best barbequed brisket sandwiches. For
dessert a fragile caramel custard with fresh berries or a
scrumptuous chocolate pecan cake. The wine list is impressive. And for lunch you can hardly go wrong with a
Smith Madrone Riesling.

The Diner, 6476 Washington Street, Yountville, (707)
944-2626; open Tuesday through Sunday for breakfast,
lunch and dinner. Just look at those old Hamilton Beach
milkshake machines. How could anyplace that still uses
those beauties not serve honest, wholesome home cooking? And that is just what The Diner does. This is my
traditional breakfast stop on my last day in the valley
before I face the drive home. The orange juice is fresh,
the French Toast excellent, the cornmeal pancakes great
and the coffee—from San Francisco's beloved Graffeo—
superb.

Now for something other than dining!

If dining is my favorite Napa Valley activity, wining is
right up there. And wine-tasting takes on the rigors of a
marathon with literally dozens of some of America's—
and the world's—great wineries welcoming you in their
tasting rooms. But two tips: let moderation be your guide
and in travelling the length of the valley try to use the
Silverado Trail rather than Highway 29—you will find it
far less congested.

Another pastime which has gained exceptional popularity in the Napa Valley also has French roots, or rather
wings. And that is hot-air ballooning. Over 200 years ago,

the brothers Montgolfier created the first hot-air balloon and a duck, a rooster and a sheep became the world's first aviators. In today's jet age, many delight in returning to this very first means of air travel in the Napa Valley. I have not been among them, but if you are interested here are a couple of firms willing to take you above terra firma: Adventures Aloft, P.O. Box 2500, Yountville, CA 94599, (707) 255-8688; Balloon Aviation of Napa Valley, 2299 Third Street, Napa, CA 94558, (707) 252-7067.

And finally, if you insist: you will find Falconcrest at 2805 Spring Mountain Road.

When your wine country stay must come to an end, head back to San Francisco by driving south on now very familiar Highway 29. At Napa pick up Highway 121 which will lead you to Highway 37, which, in turn, takes you to the Redwood Highway 101 and on to San Francisco.

After the deluxe wining and dining you have been so mercilessly subjected to for the past few days, I don't think it would be humane of me to offer you anything even remotely fancy on your return to San Francisco. So, allow me introduce you to San Francisco's Number One hamburger parlor—Bill's Place, 2315 Clement Street between 24th and 25th Avenues (221-5262; open daily from ll a.m. until 9 p.m.).

This is one of San Francisco's most beloved hamburger spots. Bill's boasts that they grind the meat fresh each day and I can believe it. But perhaps even more important is that everything tastes fresh. The healthy-sized meat patty can be had in a multitude of ways, including a burger with San Marino sauce named after Jack Shelton, the originator of this guide. Yet, I personally have always preferred the regular Cheeseburger with American Cheese. I also like my onions raw, but Bill's will gladly grill them to order at no extra charge. The French fries are a happy compromise between the thin fast-food style and those too-thick fish fries. The end potato skins are left on. And I always ask for mine to be well done. The milk shakes and malts, made from scratch with award-winning Dreyer's ice cream, are wonderfully thick but not impossible to enjoy with a straw. And the vanilla malt has enough malt in it to turn it beige. Also delicious is the ultimate Patty Melt. On a nice day, enjoy Bill's outdoor back garden bedecked with hanging flowers. It's a lovely and extremely unusual quiet retreat—especially for a for a hamburger joint! But then that's San Francisco!

To reach Bill's on your return from the Wine Country, after passing through the Toll Plaza of the Golden Gate Bridge, take the turnoff marked "19th Avenue—Golden Gate Park." After emerging from a tunnel, make a right turn at the third stop light (Clement Street), and you will reach Bill's in about ten short blocks.

Why Is San Francisco Such a Great Restaurant City?

When it comes to the quality, sheer number and variety of restaurants, San Francisco ranks second only to New York City. But when one considers the entire "restaurant experience," no city in America, not even New York, rivals the City by the Bay. Why?

Because, quite simply, San Francisco is a restaurant town. Its residents consider "restaurant going" a cultural activity in the same way New Yorkers think of their theaters. Attend a typical party here and you find the conversations often dominated by references to the latest dining-out discovery, the loss of a famous chef by another establishment, or the deterioration of a previously highly regarded dining emporium. In fact, restaurant going is such a hot topic that one local newspaper and a local magazine both have had "gossip columns" devoted strictly to restaurant news!

We San Franciscans find it easy to go out to a restaurant. Distances are short and we think nothing of popping out to a low-rent residential area to try the latest entry into Moroccan or Vietnamese cooking. We are even willing to cross a bridge or journey down the Peninsula, if we hear of a new and exciting addition to the restaurant scene. And we do all this secure in the knowledge we will not be greeted by haughty headwaiters with outstretched palms demanding a reward before granting us a table. We have little or no fear we will be subject to snobby waiters. And with the possible exception of one (Trader Vic's), special preferred sections or rooms in our restaurants are not reserved for only the very rich, or the famous, or even the regulars.

Add to this the exciting variety of ethnic foods being served and you have San Francisco—a restaurant-goer's paradise! Restaurants serving regional Chinese food other than Cantonese, such as Hunanese, Szechwan, Pekinese and Shanghai, were known here long before their national popularity; authentic Moroccan restaurants here pioneered this exotic cuisine in America; a family-run Vietnamese restaurant opened here years before this kind of cooking was even presented in New York. And, of course, the whole genre of "California cuisine," which has influenced cooking throughout the nation, was born here.

The San Francisco restaurant scene does have a few gaps. By and large, our seafood restaurants cannot compare with those of the East because the Pacific coast cannot compare with the Atlantic coast for aquatic produce; however, careful selection can go a long way to offsetting this limitation. In addition, although we have a couple of acceptable Jewish-type delicatessens, none presents the quality of hot pastrami and corned beef found only in New York. But even a greater gap is the lack of truly top-notch Italian restaurants.

Yet, unless you plan to hold a U.S. restaurant Olympics and serve as judge, you are bound to find the entire restaurant-going experience in San Francisco more satisfying than that in any other American city. It is quite possibly the last remaining American city where you can approach your selection of restaurants with the warm feeling that you will be treated courteously, that your patronage will be welcomed, and the food you order will be, in most cases, unmatched elsewhere. There are exceptions, of course. But with the copy of this book you now hold in your hands, it is hoped you will follow my personal selections and avoid them.

Index of Recommended Restaurants

This index covers all restaurants recommended in this book and, for your convenience, lists them by location and style of cuisine served. Because restaurants often change days and hours open, *you are urged to phone ahead in all cases.* And, except where they are not accepted, reservations are strongly advised. The description of the restaurant along with specific menu suggestions appear on the pages indicated in italics.

Recommended Restaurants:

Restaurants by Location:

SAN FRANCISCO:

Downtown:
Campton Place
Palm
Pierre
Plum
Post Street Bar & Cafe
Sears'
Sutter 500
Trader Vic's

Chinatown:
Golden Dragon
    Noodle Shop
Sam Wo Company
Ton Kiang
Tung Fong

Civic Center:
Hayes Street Grill
Modesto Lanzone's in
    Opera Plaza

*Financial Dist. & Lower
    Market St.:*
Garden Court
Jack's
Pier 23
Square One

Ghirardelli Sq. Area:
Buena Vista Cafe
Chez Michel
Mandarin

Modesto Lanzone's
Paprikas Fono

Nob Hill:
Crown Room
Etoile, L'

North Beach:
Tommaso's

Pier 39:
Swiss Louis

Van Ness Avenue:
House of Prime Rib
Peacock

Further Out:
Archil
Bill's Place
Castel, Le
Garden House
Greens
Khan Toke
La Rocca's
Mansour, El
Mike's Chinese
    Cuisine
Sanppo

Marin County:
Alta Mira Hotel
Casa Madrona
Horizons
Marin Joe's

Oakland:

Mexicana, La

Wine Country:

Au Relais
Diner, The
Miramonte
Mount View Hotel
Mustard's
Rhone, Le

Mendocino Coast:

Cafe Beaujolais
Little River Inn

Little River Restaurant
New Boonville

Carmel-Monterey-Big Sur

Clock Garden
Giuliano's
Nepenthe
Whaling Station

Hearst Castle:

Brambles

Yosemite:

Ahwahnee Hotel

*San Francisco, Oakland and Marin County Restaurants
by type of cuisine:*

AFTER-THEATER:

Chez Michel
Sam Wo Company
Trader Vic's

AMERICAN:

Alta Mira Hotel
Bill's Place
Buena Vista Cafe
Campton Place
Casa Madrona
Garden Court
Greens
Hayes Street Grill
Horizons
House of Prime Rib
Palm
Pier 23
Plum

Post Street Bar & Cafe
Sears'
Square One

BREAKFAST:

Buena Vista Cafe
Sears'

BUFFET:

Crown Room

CHINESE (lunch only):

Golden Dragon
Tung Fong

CHINESE (Cantonese):

Mike's Chinese Cuisine
Sam Wo Company

CHINESE (Other):
Mandarin
Ton Kiang

FRENCH:
Castel, Le
Chez Michel
Etoile, L'
Jack's
Pierre
Sutter 500

HAMBURGERS:
Bill's Place

HUNGARIAN:
Paprikas Fono

INDIAN:
Peacock

ITALIAN:
Marin Joe's
Modesto Lanzone's
Modesto Lanzone's in
    Opera Plaza
Swiss Louis
Tommaso's

JAPANESE:
Sanppo

MEXICAN:
Mexicana, La

MOROCCAN:
Mansour, El

POLYNESIAN-
CONTINENTAL:
Trader Vic's

RUSSIAN:
Archil

SEAFOOD:
Hayes Street Grill
La Rocca's

STEAKS:
Marin Joe's
Palm

THAI:
Khan Toke

VEGETARIAN:
Greens
Peacock

VIETNAMESE:
Garden House

INDEX